The Ultimate Guide to Goddess Empowerment

Other Books by Sophia

* * * * *

The Little Book of Hot Love Spells
The Little Book of Money Spells
The Magical Garden
The Little Book of Office Spells
The Little Book of Love Spells
The Little Book of Hexes for Women

Sophia's Web site:
www.psychicsophia.com

the ultimate guide to Goddess Empowerment

SOPHIA

**Andrews McMeel
Publishing**

Kansas City

The Ultimate Guide to Goddess Empowerment

03 04 05 06 07 VAI 10 9 8 7 6 5 4 3 2 1

Library of Congress-in-Publication Data

Sophia, 1955–
     The ultimate guide to goddess empowerment / Sophia.
          p. cm.
     ISBN 0-7404-3496-2
     1. Charms. 2. Magic. 3. Ritual. 4. Goddess religion. I. Title.

BF1621.S67 2003
291.2'114—dc21

2003041802

★ ★ ★ ★ ★ Attention: Schools and Businesses ★ ★ ★ ★ ★

* * * * *

This book is dedicated to all the goddess worshippers
living now and soon to come: She returns!

The Empowerments are especially dedicated to
the small goddess girls we love and adore: Angela, Brittany,
Ashley, Nichole, Lauren, Ana, Vivian, Ella, Maya, Kaija, Mitto,
Katie, Audrey, Ann, and all the rest of you!

Goddess Power Rules!

Contents

* ★ * ★ *

Acknowledgments

* * * * *

I also need to thank the following for help and support—Goddess bless them:

My patient and visionary editor, Jean Lucas; Robert Carey, the Living Encyclopedia; Joan Poor, the Priestess of Pele; Jillian Blume, the inspiration for Bast; and my husband/copy editor/playmate, Denny Sargent.

Introduction

★ ★ ★ ★ ★

For most of history, people all over the world have seen the divine in feminine form. However, over time the goddess, in all her many names and aspects, has been sometimes forgotten. As long as women continue to give to assure the continuation of our species, the goddess lives within our hearts and minds.

Over the last century the goddess has slowly but surely been reawakened in the unconscious and conscious minds of western culture. She is popping up everywhere, from the Green movement to pop music. The goddess is cool! There are millions of wonderful goddesses out there who are pulsing with power and personality and who are wonderful to play with! Why let the billions of people in Asia and Africa who worship the goddess have all the fun?

For the record, this is only a selection of goddesses, and not a complete one at that. I beg for forgiveness of all the great, exciting, and worthwhile goddesses that I have yet to meet and get to know. Sorry! Next time! I have tried to offer a selection of the most powerful and important goddesses I have encountered, from many different cultures. So many goddesses, so little time!

Why I am a goddess devotee will become clear to you as you read these pages and call these lovely deities into your hearts and homes. Maybe you're sick, sorry, damaged, or could use a break from the crazy world of spiritual machismo. Everyone should give the goddess (any goddess) a try!

Just a few words about empowerment. Each human is a divine being. Within us live the gods and goddesses, including all masks and aspects of the divine. By taking on the power of a goddess, you are connecting with and gaining power from a part of deep down inside yourself. If each of us is on this planet to "know thyself," then empowering yourself in this way can only help you evolve. It has worked for me and for others. We are all divine, but we have forgotten how wonderful, creative, and amazing each of us really is! *The Ultimate Guide to Goddess Empowerment* helps you rediscover these things, one goddess at a time.

At the beginning of each chapter is a list of important key attributes for each goddess. This includes the origin, or culture, from which the goddess came from, the attributes of that goddess or what the main powers of that goddess are, the color, symbol, element, stone or metal, and scent. In some cases, I contacted the goddess herself and asked her what she likes!

So how can you use these? If you need to protect children or pets, call upon Artemis. Since she likes silver it would be a good idea to wear lots of silver jewelry, including a crescent moon. You should wear silver clothing if you can, burn pine incense, and maybe wear jewelry made from moonstones. These things are all sacred to her, so if you want to invite her to visit, all of them will make her feel welcome. You may also want to make a small altar to her with a silver cloth, some pine boughs, a silver cup of spring water, and an image of her as well as an arrow or an image of one. Again, these are all sacred to her, so she will more likely bless you if you offer her what she likes.

If you need love, call upon the Roman Goddess Venus. She likes the colors green, red, and pink, so use these colors for an altar cloth, or wear that color lingerie, like her enchanted girdle. Venus loves roses, so if you want to attract love into your life, put roses in a vase to get her attention. Wear a piece of jewelry that is sacred to her, be it gold, copper, turquoise, or emeralds. Sometimes just lighting up a candle or incense that Venus would find pleasing is enough to have her raise an eyebrow in your direction. When you call on the goddess of love, she will answer.

If you desire prosperity, call upon Lakshmi. Since she likes gold, you can wear a simple gold chain to invoke her and bring wealth into your life, or cover your entire altar in gold cloth, gold candles, or gold chocolate coins for a more dramatic effect. Either way, you will attract her attention and she will love to come and pay you a visit, bringing you the opportunities for real wealth.

It is important to remember that you do not have to go to great lengths to become a goddess. You can simply wear her color, her scent, or even a piece of sacred jewelry. Sometimes a little goddess goes a long way!

By the way, this goes for *all* goddesses. If a good friend of yours came to visit and she loved red wine and Miles Davis, what would you serve her? What music would you play? Exactly!

Now, let's talk about the different goodies in each chapter. After the list of attributes, you will find an introduction. Think of this as a sort of goddess résumé. This gives you the history, myths, stories, and forms of that goddess. It is good to know who you are inviting into your space, don't you think? It is advisable to check this out before playing with a goddess. Some people simply do not get along well; the same goes for mortals and goddesses. Be polite and be respectful and all will be well—but it also never hurts to have some advance information.

The next section of each chapter is the invocation. This is a neat "call" to the goddess and can be used anytime and anywhere you like. It stands alone, meaning you can use it as you like, and it doesn't have to be combined with anything else. Sometimes I just want to dance naked under the stars, drink champagne, and call to a goddess with some lovely poetry—don't you? Well, for these and any other special occasion, the invocations are perfect. Be creative! Burn a little incense that the goddess likes! Make a little altar with her symbol, an image of her and some offerings. Then launch that invocation and have some impromptu fun. You go, girl!

The next section is the visualization exercise. Each Goddess Empowerment Visualization is a way to "meet" the particular goddess in her world, the world of higher spiritual vibration and dreams, sometimes called the astral plane.

Ideally, you close your eyes and relax your mind when you do these visualizations. You may read the visualization you wish to do ahead of time and remember the steps as you relax, but it may be easier and more effective to tape the visualization exercise text ahead of time and then listen to it as you are lying down with your eyes closed. Or you could have someone quietly read it to you as you relax with your eyes closed.

In preparation, lie in a quiet, dark place where you will not be disturbed for at least twenty minutes.

You may wish to set up that goddess's image, burn a candle and some incense to her, and wear comfortable ritualistic clothes. Wear clothes that the particular goddess you are becoming would find pleasing, and always make sure that you adorn yourself with her colors of power. Goddess visualizations can also be done in bed before you go to sleep if you wish to work with a goddess in dreamtime. When you "come back" from your visualization, take time to adjust. Breathe deeply and lie still for a few minutes before getting up and doing some activity. Make sure you are well grounded, and thank the goddess before returning to "normal" consciousness. Visualizations can be done by yourself but are much more fun to do with a group of people, even men. Try leading a whole group of friends onto the astral plane to meet a fun goddess! Now that's a party!

Each chapter ends with the big one, the Goddess Empowerment Ritual. This takes some preparation, some thought, and a lot of energy. It also is the most fun and wonderful part of each chapter, because it is with the empowerments that you can become each goddess! Why ask for love or money when you can become love or money? Think about that!

I do have a few things to say about these empowerments though. First of all, get to know your goddess before you do the empowerment. It is really like having someone over to your house. Read the introduction, get her scent, her symbol, an image of the goddess (it could be a picture, a drawing, or a small statue), some flowers that fit her, some food she'd like, and so on. Put these all on a small altar before you do the empowerment. Treat her as an honored guest.

When you do an empowerment, don't be in a hurry, don't be sloppy about it, and make sure you are not disturbed. Prepare yourself for the ritual like you would for a big date or big event. Primp. Get lovely. Wear the right colors, the right metal or stone, and the right symbol for the goddess if you can. Get in the mood. If the empowerment calls for specific things, they belong on the altar. If the ritual doesn't say exactly what to do with these items, relax. They are offerings and a focus for the goddess. It is traditional to offer flowers, food, drink, and so on to the goddess. These should be eaten afterward or left for animals outside.

It is also important to note that more than one person can do these empowerments at a time, and that includes men. There are a lot of men out there who are potential or actual goddess worshippers, and since you are a goddess, isn't that a nice thought? If you decide to do an empowerment with others, simply read the ritual together. These empowerments are great fun to do with groups. I've used them in this way many times. What a party!

A word about fire in rituals, especially outside: *Be careful!* You are honoring the goddess, and Nature is very much a part of the goddess. Start a fire and you lose all goddess privileges for the next few lifetimes. Use candles (of that goddess's color, of course!) and make sure they are in candle holders. Outside, put them in candle lanterns. Don't ever burn a candle in the woods if there is any sort of fire risk: Use your common sense! A small mirror can easily replace a candle symbolically in a ritual, and so can a flashlight.

Each empowerment goes like this: The sacred space is created. The real action then begins with you calling the goddess into your magical circle and into your self. It then progresses so that you become and speak as the goddess. Be ready for this heavy shift; remember, you are a goddess. Accept the goddess with perfect love and perfect trust, and all will be well, never fear! Yet, as with all magic, it is also a good idea to think the whole thing through and carefully prepare before you do it.

At a certain point, each empowerment says something like "when you return to being you . . ." This simply means that when the power of the goddess you have called upon leaves you, you will have a period of time when you return to your normal state of consciousness. Take a few moments to "come down" from the bliss of being a goddess. Relax. Get grounded. Then finish the empowerment.

I want to add that these empowerments are to be fun, but they are also powerful and real. Feel free to add some personal touches. You now know what scents, color, and other things each goddess likes, so have fun with it! You can also do a little divination near the end of each empowerment if you like: Create some art, play music, whatever is appropriate for you and that goddess. Don't be frivolous, but do be creative.

After you finish an empowerment, take a walk or a nap, or do something calm and meditative so you can really savor the experience. It is always a good idea to keep a journal of these things. Amazing thoughts will come to you! You will be utterly amazed at what goddess power can do to help you and improve your life.

So go for the gold! Decide what power you need and become that power. Live, learn, and have fun! Need better luck? Call upon the goddess Fortuna! Need a little tender loving care? The goddess Tara will help! Is your love life in the dumps? The goddess Venus lives to bring you romance! Think of these goddesses as really fun, really powerful girl-friends. Each is only a magical moment away.

Empower yourself, and become the goddess you dream to be! Take control of your life and rule your world. But, as the goddess says, play hard, but play fair, and always have fun!

Sophia
Goddess-in-training

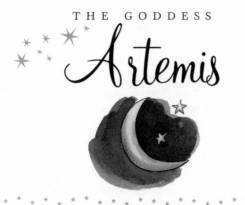

THE GODDESS
Artemis

ORIGIN: Greek
ATTRIBUTES: protection for children and animals
COLOR: silver
SYMBOLS: bow and arrow, crescent moon
ELEMENT: air
STONE/METAL: moonstone or silver
SCENT: pine

INTRODUCTION

Need a kick-ass goddess to protect your kids, your animals, or the wilderness and wildlife you love? Artemis has been doing this for ages! Call on this powerful, young, strong moon goddess to protect all the little ones in your life.

Goddess of the moon, Apollo's sister Artemis is one of the most beloved and persistent of the Greek goddesses. She is best known as a perpetually youthful goddess, one who lives and moves totally independent of men. Her name means "strong-limbed, she who cuts up, or water from above." She carries with her a sacred silver bow and quiver of arrows, and is in every way a wild warrioress.

Her home is found in all mountains and wild places. She is the patroness of all wild animals as well as being the goddess who watches over childbirth and children. She is the triple-aspected moon goddess who is also the daughter of Zeus and Leto. When Zeus asked Artemis what divine powers she wanted, she replied that she wanted many of the things he had mentioned previously to her as well as the ability to bring light, hunting accouterments, and many nymphs to help out.

She roamed the mountains of Greece, and in Arcadia had a famous congress with the god Pan, who gave her divine hounds. They became her symbol and her helpers. She also found and tamed two sacred horned deer and used them to pull her glowing golden chariot.

She seems to have archaic connections with ancient Cretan goddesses and a number of small local goddesses. She is identified as the primordial bear goddess Ursa, also a constellation known as the Big Dipper. There is a connection between Ursa and the later Celtic bear goddess Artio, who is also linked with Artemis. In any event, her worship spread far and wide, and today a number of Wiccans, neo-pagans, and others have revived her worship and hear her hunting horn.

Artemis is invoked because she is the mistress of the wild and protector of the innocent, especially children and animals. She hunts, but much as other animals hunt, as the goddess of cycles. May this wild goddess, patroness of these wild places, help to stop the exploitation of children, animals, and the wilderness, and empower us to protect those things as well!

* * * * *

Invocation of Artemis

Glorious maiden of the silver moon
Lady of the silver bow
Power and joy are your arrows
Great warrior goddess, we call upon you now.
You who fly across the mountains and valleys
You who tread the places wild and wonderful
You who shine the silver radiance of truth.
Protection
And the living energy of all wild animals

Come! Hear my plea
Protect your children!
Protect all the wild animals
Protect the wild places and all nature!
We call thee with the voices of a worried parent
With the howl of the threatened wolf, the speared whale,
The falling eagle, the tortured tiger!
Hear now, through our prayer
Our need and swiftly come
Bring now the power to help and protect
Place in my hands your sacred silver bow of the sun
Your magick arrows of the stars
That I may be your instrument
That I may protect my wild brothers and sisters
Your children, in flesh and cloaked in fur and feather.
Artemis! Fill our heads, our hearts, our spirits
With the primal wild-lust for life
Your pitiless willpower and deep insight
That we can do what needs be done!
Protect us
Help us
Inspire us!
We invoke thee as the primal huntress
Striding through the dark green forests by starlight
Sacred hounds baying at thy heels
Silver crown on your head
Black onyx gleam in your eyes.
Great bear mother Artio!
Make all know this!
That every child
Every animal friend
Is protected by you
That all fauna are brother and sister
And then dance in the silver veil for them.

We invoke the great Goddess Artemis
She of the million breasts

Streaming milk and life to all living animals.
She of the million faces
Turned toward all living things with the silver-green power
Inciting growth and nourishing
Artemis all-mother.
Through us begin the healing
Through us protect and save all endangered children
Be the strength of our arms and the gleam in our eyes.
Guard the hatchlings, the foals, the cubs, and the infants.

With your power may we help to protect all children
With your love may we shelter and care for all
Animal friends
With your wild warrior hear.

Heiros Artemis!

* * * * *

$\mathcal{G}$ODDESS ARTEMIS VISUALIZATION EXERCISE

You are hovering amidst a wild place
One that has drawn you, a special place for you.
You feel the webs of life, the woven life energies,
You see and feel the trees, bushes, plants, and flowers.
The birds, mammals, and reptiles are familiar
Until your energy encompasses this wild place.
You speak with your mind to all living animals,
Your love drains the fear from them.
You show them that most humans do love them,
You see them, with your help, hide and escape all hunters.
You protect them with your expanded aura,
See the endangered animals protected by this white aura,
See the wild animals grow stronger, more numerous,
See those like you, all beaming white energy around the globe.
These energies become a web, joining together.
Feed them more energy and see them succeed.
You feel one with the wild place and it is now dawn.

See the borders of your personal energy field
To the North, West, South, and East.
Connect many other protecting energy fields,
Feel the green glowing circle of your center.
The energy from this ripples out to fill the circled wild place,
In the center of this wild place is a Home,
It is every home.
It is the place where every child lives,
You see there the world's children,
Innocent,
Vulnerable,
And you see a silver moonlight-cloth covering them,
The cloak of Artemis,
Shielding them from all harm!
Her sphere of silver light expands,
This sphere becomes a giant globe of silver,
Covering, protecting, hiding.

Your wild place and all the children and animals within it
You see that bad humans cannot enter it to do damage,
You see that poisons are kept away from it,
The life energy is green and strong within it
This area is safe and protected.
At each quarter and over your head you see crescent moons glowing,
Keeping this land safe by the goddess power of children and wild
    places.
Deep silent prayers come to you to seal the barrier,
The many-colored emanations of these ripple out and merge,
With the circle of light protecting the place.
A special ray of energy touches those children and animals who are
    in danger
That they may prosper and be safe
In freedom and joy
And the silver light of Artemis.

*G*RAND EMPOWERMENT RITUAL OF ARTEMIS FOR PROTECTING THE INNOCENT

This rite is to become Artemis the wild huntress, to become the great moon goddess and protector of all the innocent children and animals. Become her and you will be giving constant love and protection to all those around you. How wonderful is that?

Go to a wild place you love (even if it's in your backyard). Bring an image, picture, symbol, or totem of the moon goddess, as well as pictures of children you love, animals, or any other beings or places needing the goddess's protection.

You Will Need

◉ white wine or water in a silver cup

◉ an arrow

◉ a rattle

◉ a yellow or "golden" apple

◉ some glue or tape

◉ some pine branches

The Ritual

During a full moon, place all these items out, including the symbol of Artemis and your personal picture(s). Make the place holy by pouring wine in the four directions and at the center, saying:

> *Heiros! Here is to the spirits, gods, and ancestors*
> *By the arrow of Artemis, the power of my will*
> *And the green power of Wilderness*
> *I do cleanse, offer, and consecrate*
> *This a place of power, a gate between the worlds*
> *A place of earth magick!*
> *Kyria!*

Show the arrow to each direction. See the space around your sacred place fill with the images of all those animals you love. All the wild and beautiful animals that need protection, all the innocent children that need your help, they give you their strength. You give them your love, saying:

Here is the truth
Here is the truth
Here is the truth
Here, now
I invoke the heart of all wild things
I invoke the voices, the souls
The glowing mind of all wild things
Here, now, is the truth!
Heiros!

Walk three times clockwise about the circle, bringing the wild power to you. Set the arrow in the center of where you have all your things displayed. Then pour out a little wine, saying:

Offerings to the wildlife
Here are my tears to heal you.
Offerings to the children
Here is my blood to empower you.
Offerings to the kin of fur and feather
Here is my rite, to bring you long life!
Io! Artemis! Kyria!

Sit, kneel, or squat. Meditate as you will. Close your eyes.

See the crescent moon before you, filling you with light and power. You are becoming Artemis, with bow and arrows, silver light about you! When the power is moving within and without, see yourself in your mother's womb. See how you developed there, see how you went through every evolutionary stage, from single cell to fish to amphibian to reptile to mammal. As you remember your link to all animals, chant:

Seed to beast
Seed to beast
I am the large
And very least.

Begin to dance slowly, using the rattle, turning on an axis, spinning as you evolve until you become the animal. Now begin to stalk about the circle, becoming a primal animal yourself. Dance in a spiral moving outward, stalking, pouncing, slithering.

And as you do so, play with all your brothers and sisters, the innocent children, all the wild animals of the forest, of your mind, and of the world. As you embrace each one, let it into your heart: Become that animal. Let it become you and dance again and again.

As you move outward, the spiral will take you deeper into the wilderness, until you reach a point where the visions stop coming. Then shake your rattle and speak:

> *I am Artemis! Wild huntress of the silver moon! Hear now me!*
> *I am every wild one*
> *I am satyr, the animal-soul*
> *I am nymph, the animal spirit*
> *This is my will . . .*
> *Heiros . . . heiros . . . heiros . . .*

Pick up the arrow in one hand, the rattle in the other. Slowly circle again, this time visualizing all the beings you wish to protect with your silver light and arrows of power. As you do this, send your protection out with every shake of your rattle, saying:

> *Protect, empower, heal*
> *With this chant*
> *I make it real!*
> *Euligia bios!*

Return to the center. Now is the time of meditation and balance. Drink the wine and eat the apple. Bring the power down, become yourself again and say

> *So it is and so be free*
> *I so will*
> *So mote it be!*
> *Io io evoe!*

Shake the rattle to the four directions, repeating this chant.

Pour the last of the wine to the four directions, repeating this chant.

Show the arrow to the four directions, repeating this chant, then stick it into the earth, saying:

> *Heal the Earth, rebirth!*

Depart and do the work. Tape or glue the symbol of Artemis on the back of your picture(s), and place the picture(s) in your home. Leave the pine branches behind for an offering. Now keep the arrow as a protective amulet. Hang it where you need protection or give it to someone else who does.

THE GODDESS
Athena

* * * * * * * * * * * * * * * * * * * *

ORIGIN: Greek
ATTRIBUTES: learning, teaching, and careers
COLOR: white/silver
SYMBOL: owl, shield
ELEMENT: air
STONE/METAL: hematite
SCENT: olive or lavender

* * * * * * * * * * * * * * * * * * * *

INTRODUCTION

Want to be a teacher? Are you in the midst of important studies or a career that calls for a clever and intelligent mind? Wish to be more erudite and scholarly? Call upon the wise Goddess Athena to sharpen your mind and fill you with learning!

The great Goddess Pallas Athena is one of the major Olympian deities of the ancient Greek pantheon. Her mother was Metis, the principle of divine law, wisdom, and foresight, who was entirely absorbed into the person of Zeus, king of the gods. He then subsequently gave birth to Athena from his head. When it was time for her to be born, Zeus cried out in pain, and his son, Hephaistos the smith-god, split open his skull with a double ax. Athena, fully grown, armored in gold and bearing shield and spear, leaped forth into the company of Mount Olympus. When carried to the mainland in Greece years later, she assumed a martial character, and her role as protector of the household expanded to become guardian of the entire city. Athena was the personification of wise counsel, a guardian of humanity, and her own city of Athens, and a guide of many of the epic heroes. She taught all the most important skills and so she became the patroness of teachers, students, craftspeople, and all who learn.

She was guardian of artists and architects, and all the arts of civilization were hers. Although she later became a goddess of battle and warfare, a great warrior and protector, hers was never the raging battle frenzy of the war-god Ares, but the discipline and skill of a fully trained and well led army. Among her symbols are the owl, a bird of wisdom that hunts by night and a powerful magickal armor called the *aegis,* of complex origin. This is said to be the goatlike skin of an evil titan, slain in battle by Athena, and ornamented with the severed head of the serpent-haired Medusa, whose gaze turned men to stone. The aegis is often depicted on the breastplate of the goddess, and it is supposedly the invisible aura of her protection. It is in her role as giver of wisdom that we associate her with the power to teach the knowledge of a culture. Education is the sharpest sword we possess and the key to all!

* * * * *

$\mathcal{I}$NVOCATION OF ATHENA

Athena! Athena! Athena!
Eulogia heiros pangenetira!
Thrice exalted we invoke you,
Great goddess of wisdom and knowledge,
Spear-maiden armored in shining gold!
Teach now your wisdom to all men and women,
To guard and guide all!
Pallas Athena, fair and serene,
Watching over all nations of the world
From the mountain Olympus where the high gods dwell,
Set your shield over the globe!
Grant me the power of education

The sharpness of a bright mind!
Your mother is Metis, teller of truth,
Eternal giver of wise counsel;
Primal goddess of right order
Who sets boundaries in the beginning
Like the ocean whose tides and purple waves
Encircle all the lands.
Your father is Zeus the thunderer,
High heaven's lord and king of the gods,
Victorious over the titans
With lightning in his hand;
From his throne on high he judges
The works and fates of humanity.
Full formed in his mind
You sprang from his brow,
Wisdom incarnate of the divine
Who knows all secrets and ever tells truth.
With the double ax Hephaistos your brother
Frees you to the wonder of the world!
Armed with shield and spear,
Garbed in golden glory,
You rise like dawn above the horizon
To guard the world from ignorance.
Grant me the power of education
The sharpness of a bright mind!
Athena polis!
Great goddess of the sacred city,
Protector of the wisdom of the people
And teacher of the generations,
Watch over me in my learning
And bring me through knowledge to wisdom;
Set your shield over the schools of the young
And guide all students to truth.
Grant me the power of education
The sharpness of a bright mind!
Athena Ergane!

Teacher of the ancient crafts,
Arts and history
Mathematics and philosophy
All sciences!
Who gives skill to the worker's hand;
Guard and guide our work of mind and art,
The pen that writes and the press that prints,
So the knowledge may spread
In all the cities, in all the towns.
Grant me the power of education
The sharpness of a bright mind!
Pallas Athena!
To save the world from ignorance!
Grant me the power of education
The sharpness of a bright mind!
Heiros Metis! Empower the mind!

★ ★ ★ ★ ★

GODDESS ATHENA VISUALIZATION EXERCISE

Beyond the green darkness and silence
Feel yourself ascending
Toward the vastness of space
That embraces the blue-green globe of earth
Wrapped in her robe of clouds and ocean.
Move like a meteor through
The ever-unfolding layers of atmosphere,
Circling ever nearer to her.
Become like a bird,
Soaring over the green hillsides
And the wild wide forests,
Over the seas and rivers and bays,
Drawing near to a deep harbor
Surrounded by a great city full of life,
A city of white marble and tall golden towers,
With streets full of life and bustling marketplaces.

At the center of this city is a broad hillside.
Crowned with an enormous temple.
On a square base, steps lead up to a vast colonnade,
Tall columns surrounding an open-roofed courtyard.
Within this sanctuary stands a great statue
Of the Goddess Pallas Athena,
Many times taller than a man,
Armored in bright gold,
Her calm face shadowed by a tall-plumed helmet.
She holds spear and shield,
And her breastplate is the aegis,
A magickal garment like a goatskin
Bearing the face of serpent-haired Medusa;
She whose gaze turns men to stone,
She who guards the mysteries of learning
Athena is aware of your presence:
The gray eyes of the all-seeing goddess
Fall upon you, clear and bright;
You feel that she knows you
As your own mother knows.
You feel the warmth of love, and more:
An understanding of all things under the sky,
The ways and workings of the world,
The wonder of it all.

Knowledge floods through you like a tidal wave
Of arts and sciences and skills,
Of writings sacred and profane;
The works of teachers and builders,
Researchers and philosophers and statesmen,
Historians and priests, poets and lovers.
The crystalline seeds of all the world's cultures
Are being planted inside your being, carried within your soul.
Wisdom flowers in your mind,
Secrets fill you faster than you can comprehend them,
But deep in your memory they remain,
And you will have all the knowledge you need

When the time is ripe.
It is a drunkenness like the wine
Of the gardens of the sun;
It is a light filling every darkness
And understanding beyond mere words.
It is the wisdom of the goddess
And the collective memory of humanity,
And can never be taken from you.
Bathe in the golden light for a time,
Drinking deep;
And then fall away,
Back into your body,
And breathe in silence for a time.

★ ★ ★ ★ ★

GRAND EMPOWERMENT RITUAL OF ATHENA: BECOMING THE POWER OF KNOWLEDGE AND LEARNING

Before performing this ritual, take time to immerse yourself in meditation, discussion, and practical work. Widen communication and networking with friends and professional coworkers. Dedicate yourself to learning, teaching, and finding solutions. Identify yourself as one who teaches and learns!

Greek rituals traditionally began with a procession to the sacred site, led by a young priestess bearing the offerings and tools in a basket. She was followed by the participants, family and friends, and accompanied by a flute player. All gathered in a circle, to be ceremonially purified by the washing of hands. Prayer and invocation would follow, and then the priestess made the offerings and sacrifice, which became a communal meal. The rite ended with loud cries as everyone scattered.

Try to find a suitable and powerful site overlooking your city or town (within the bounds of privacy and discretion). If you must do it indoors, do so in a library or place of study and have all the windows open with sunlight filling the room.

You Will Need

◎ a basket

◎ an image or symbol of the Goddess Athena

◎ a simple flute or pennywhistle

◎ flowers

◎ matches

◎ a gold candle

◎ some olive oil

◎ a ceramic cup

◎ some spring water

◎ incense (frankincense is best)

◎ wine

◎ foods like bread and olives

The Ritual

Fill the basket with all the other items. Proceed to the site with the basket. Place the image or symbol of Athena on top of the basket and focus on it, and play a simple tune on the flute. Find your sacred sun-filled spot and scatter the flowers around you, say:

> I stand here to worship Athena,
> Great lady of wisdom and power,
> Guardian of the cities of humanity.
> I ask her aid that the word may be heard,
> That wisdom may spread to city and town,
> To farmland and forest, around the globe
> That I may become the fire of that wisdom
> That I may be filled by the word of knowing
> Eulogia heiros Athena!

Light the candle. Anoint it, your temples, and your forehead with olive oil, saying:

> Pallas Athena!
> The olive tree was your gift to us,
> And in your name
> I kindle its flame!
> Let the light of your wisdom

Dawn upon the world,
So that I may see clearly the truth.
That I may become the fire of that wisdom
That I may be filled by the word of knowing
Io evoe!

Now fill the cup with water. Carry it around in a circle, then pour water over your hands, saying:

Let the waters of life and memory
Wash me clean of the dust of the mundane
That I may come to speak with the goddess
In a sacred place of purity and peace!

Light the incense and wave it to each of the four directions and call the four elements:

We call upon Euros,
The wind of the East,
To witness this rite.
Spread the word of wisdom
That I may lean and teach!

We call upon Notos,
The wind of the South,
To witness this rite.
Spread the word of wisdom
That I may learn and teach!

We call upon Zephyros,
The wind of the West,
To witness this rite.
Spread the word of wisdom
That I may learn and teach!

We call upon Boreas,
The wind of the North,
To witness this rite.
Spread the word of wisdom
That I may learn and teach!

Stand in the center of the circle and say:

Here is the place of truth
Where wise counsel may be heard
In the voice of Pallas Athena
And in my heart.
I call on the great goddess
To guard me and to guide me.
Heiros heiros heiros!

Now is the time to become the goddess of wisdom!

Pour wine into the cup filled with water. As they mix, feel the power and spirit of the goddess cover you, saying:

Pallas Athena! I sing your song!
I am thee! Heiros Gamos!
I am wine and memory,
Incense burns in my name!
I embody wisdom, shield all with truth,
So the earth may grow strong
For the generations to come!
Eulogia heiros
I am Athena!

Drink the wine-water and feel the energies fill you. See through Her eyes! Your mind is filled! Say:

Let truth be heard!
Awaken the world!
Make strong the land!
I am the owl of all intellect!
I am the fire of wisdom!
I am the word of knowing!
Kyria Athena . . . kyria Athena . . . ! (repeat as desired)

Visualize an ever widening circle of light spreading from the incense at the center of the circle. The light is *you,* expanding to cover the globe. Then sit in silence for a time.

See yourself learning and teaching in the world with the power of Athena. Open yourself to messages, omens, and teachings from the goddess.

When you return to being "you," finish the wine-water and pour out a few drops in thanks to the goddess, saying:

I give thanks to the great goddess,
Who gives teachings of wisdom
And guards the knowledge
Of all living things!
We give thanks to the four winds,
Who have warded our rite:
Euros, wind of the East,
We thank you!
Notos, wind of the South,
We thank you!
Zephyros, wind of the West,
We thank you!
Boreas, wind of the North,
We thank you!

Eulogia heiros Athena!
May wisdom rule! Iao!

Enjoy the food that you have brought, and then depart and do the work in all the world.

THE GODDESS Bast

ORIGIN: Egyptian
ATTRIBUTES: joy, pleasure, and protecting cats
COLOR: pink or gold
SYMBOL: cat or sistrum
ELEMENT: fire
STONE/METAL: tiger's-eye
SCENT: patchouli

INTRODUCTION

Bast is an ancient Egyptian goddess usually shown as a regal cat with sacred symbols and jewelry. Bast brings us pleasure, hedonistic delight, erotic fun, and joy for life! This sexy Egyptian goddess is the wild cat in all of us who loves to do nothing more than dance the night away. She is the goddess of music, pleasure, and sexuality. Think of a beautiful girl with the mask of a cat, with skin or fur that's black, white, or yellow.

Bast's origin can be traced to the wildcats that lived in the swamps around the Nile River. Later they became domesticated cats that guarded the grain warehouses. Thus the Egyptians worshipped cats because they were the guardians of their food as well as being beautiful and mysterious. Because of the role these cats played in saving grain, bread and beer are also associated with Bast, the carefree, loving goddess. Cats were so sacred in Egypt that no one was allowed to take them out of the kingdom.

The Greeks identified Bast with Artemis, mother of the nine muses. This is where the legend that all cats have nine lives comes from. Bast Temple was at the city of Bubastis in the delta region, where a necropolis has been found containing mummified cats.

Sacred to her is the *sistrum*, a sort of a metal rattle used in ancient rituals. Also sacred to her are all cats (of course!), sensuous fun, and alcoholic beverages. The colors associated with Bast are pink, like a cat's tongue, or the gold of the rising sun. Her scent and herb are patchouli and catnip. Some of Her other sacred symbols are baskets and the ankh.

The famous Greek historian Herodotus said Bast's temple was the most beautiful temple in Egypt. It was elaborately decorated with carved figures and surrounded by two canals that were fed by the Nile. Above the temple was a large shrine, which contained the statue of the Goddess Bast. The road leading to the temple was lined on both sides with immense trees, so tall that they seemed to touch the sky.

Bast is also a sun goddess, because her father was the Sun God Ra. Bast is identified with the sun especially at dawn, when the sun is at its softest part of the day. Bast is sometimes called "Lady of the East" and "The Lightbearer." Interestingly enough, Bast is also called a moon goddess, since cats can see at night, and their eyes glow like a full moon. Black cats were especially sacred to Bast, and ancient Egyptian physicians used the symbol for the black cat in healing.

Bast has a playful, fun-loving, sexy side. Any ritual for her should always be joyful. Bast is the goddess of music, dance, and the arts. The priestesses of Bast were known for their erotic dance ritual, the forerunner of modern erotic dance and stripping. If you need joy, pleasure, and music in your life, then the Goddess Bast is for you.

* * * * *

$\mathcal{G}$ODDESS BAST INVOCATION

Beautiful feline goddess,
Like a cat you come into
My temple.

Softly you fill my temple
Like perfume of the sun.
Dominatrix of all your domain,
You are a fierce wildcat.
The powerful and pleasure loving
Bast! Great goddess,
Bring pleasure and plenty
Enjoyment and music!
You mark your territory
With your rub against
What you desire.
I invoke you, Lady of
Light, when the sun is at
Its most benign
At dawn.
Softly you warm
The earth this sunrise.
Breath of joy
Flame of passion
Sacred one of the earth.
Af An Nuteru Bast!

Bast, you are also
A moon goddess
Lady of Night
Temptress of Silver.
The pale moonlight is
Reflected in your eyes,
At night you get visions
The stars also are seen in your eyes
O Great Black Cat!
Tua Bubastis!

A musical goddess are you
Playing music and dancing
You bring us the striptease!
Each veil a world of sensation

Each thought a flame
In your eyes!
Bring us good times!
Bring us beer, wine,
Bread is sacred to you.
I receive pleasure!
Heka em Bast!

You watched over the
Grain and made sure
That it was protected
From creatures not wanted
And so protect our food!
Our cats!
Our pleasures!

A lovely cat goddess are you
Your fur comes in many colors,
Some long, some short,
You come in all colors.

Some see you as a young woman
With the face of a cat,
Your twin is Sekhmet,
The sister with the lioness mask.

I call upon the pleasure,
Fun, and play of Bast
The party goddess of them all
With this invocation of joy
I call you Great Cat Mother!
Tua Bast!

It is with this invocation that
I summon up play.
Let all dance wildly to music
And to drink and feast
From when the moon rises
Until dawn begins the next day.

Hail to you, cat goddess!
Heka em Bast!

* * * * *

$\mathcal{G}$ODDESS BAST VISUALIZATION EXERCISE

You see a black cat, emissary of the cat goddess.
She is a black cat, wearing gold, walking in the desert.
Now, walk to Bubastis, the ancient city of the lady Bast.
The cat will lead you to her temple.
In front of you see two canals
The water is from the Nile
Its gentle currents sweep around an island
Like a sand castle
Right in front the water stops.
Walk across the drawbridge
Many trees surround the large building,
Cats everywhere, in the trees and on the ground.
The gateway is tall and seems to touch the sun
It is decorated with carved figures . . . cats!
As you walk past the cats, one walks up to you and rubs it head,
    body, and tail
You reach down to pet it and the cat winks at you and then walks
    toward the city.
Its tail twitching in the air
The cat turns around to see if you are coming and you do.
Walking behind the cat, you start to follow.
The temple stands in the center of the city,
And as you walk around you notice that all the buildings have been
    raised.
The temple is before you!
Pillars glowing, gold everywhere
Lotus flowers and cat sculptures
And a light inside like the sun.
You climb the many steps and enter the coolness
Of the inner shrine

Before you is Bast!
A beautiful black cat seated upon a throne of gold
You look into her eyes and they become bigger,
And suddenly you are in her green eyes
A warm ocean of pleasure
Sensory joy
And ecstasy!
Float within this warm sea as long as you like.
When you return
You are curled up,
Purring like a cat,
And her slinking image disappears—
Winking!

* ★ * ★ *

Goddess Bast Empowerment Ritual: Calling Forth Fun and Pleasure

This is where you get to become the great powerful Bast, the cat goddess of joy and fun. With this empowerment, leave your cares at the door and move on to the joyfulness of life. Like any ritual, this empowerment should be respectful of your inner goddess, but Bast's lighthearted approach to life should get you moving to the beat and pointed in the right direction toward enjoyment.

You Will Need

◎ a basket
◎ a bell
◎ matches
◎ a pink candle
◎ patchouli incense or oil
◎ seven beautiful scarves or veils that you wear around you
(These are the only things, aside from jewelry, that you wear!)
◎ a CD of your favorite music
◎ a CD player
◎ a statue of Bast

◉ some pink flowers and sweets (optional)

◉ dark beer (or, if you do not drink, catnip tea)

The Ritual

Close the curtains and go to the sunniest location in your home. Place all the items in the basket and set up everything facing south. Do this rite soon after dawn. Have cat things about. Wear any cat prints you have and amber jewelry, if you have it.

Ring the bell all around the space, clockwise. Light the candle and incense, saying:

> *Cat mother*
> *Bast, Bubastis, Pasht!*
> *Heka em Bast!*
> *Sa Sekhem Neter Bast!*
> *Bast*
> *Lady of the sun and moon*
> *Goddess of pleasure and joy*
> *Come now!*
> *Join this feast of pleasure!*
> *Fill me with your warm heat*
> *Heka*
> *Heka*
> *Heka Bast!*

Now face the North, hit the bell, and say:

> *I am Bast*
> *Hear me purr*
> *Do not rub my fur the wrong way*
> *Of that you can be sure*
> *Tua Bast!*

Now face the East, hit the bell, and say:

> *Lady of the East*
> *Kitty savant of the dawn*
> *Your father was Ra the sun king*
> *Who watches over all*
> *Tua Bast*

Now face the South, hit the bell, and say:

I salute the Goddess Bast
The slyest one of all
I welcome you goddess
To entertain one and all
Tua Bast

Now face the West, hit the bell, and say:

The moon has risen
I can see it in your eyes
When I see into the night
I have night vision
Tua Bast

Now sit in the center, hit the bell, and say:

Goddess Bast
Of the four corners
Goddess of pleasure of fun
With this empowerment
Enjoyment will be done
Tua Bast

Now, anoint yourself at the temples, heart, and lower belly with the perfume or oil. Drape the seven veils around you. Put on your hot music and dance! Dance a sensuous dance and as you do, take off each veil and toss it, saying "Tua Bast!" each time. Get into the sexy hip-hop or whatever kind of music turns you on. Heck, even country-western music is okay. Bast is the goddess of music and pleasure, so do not be shy. Shake it, baby! Do your wild striptease!

When naked, become the goddess! Let her energy fill you! Say:

I am the Cat Goddess Bast!
I am lovely and lithe
I move across the dance floor
And all eyes are upon me
I slink around
I can leap over buildings
Hide underground
I am slight of figure

And am one of grace
I am the Goddess Bast
The cat goddess
I am a cat!
Pleasure
Joy
Grace
Power
Seduction
Stalking!
Heka Heka Heka
Bast!
I am feline joy
Of play not prey
The one who
Worships fun
Enjoyment and parties
Especially at night
I am Bast!
I prowl the world
Bring joy!
I am the Goddess Bast
I am the mistress of cats
I am the queen of music
I am the pleasure diva
I am the predator of the night
I have the reflection of light in my eyes
Dancing and partying is all that I do
All night and in the day I sleep
I am the Goddess Bast
The queen of the party
The kitty cat that reigns
Over a good time for all
Heka
Heka
Bast am I!

Now that you are undressed, congratulate yourself on a job well done. Place the statue of Bast on top of the basket and surround the basket with pink flowers and sweets. Sit down and have a drink of the beer or catnip tea. Become the goddess of pleasure. Stretch! Purr! Whisper:

> *I am the Goddess Bast*
> *I will have a great time*
> *Pleasure without shame*
> *I will dance my cares away*
> *Not a worry have I*
> *Nothing can go wrong*
> *I am a cat on the prowl*

Now, take a very short catnap and let Bast's energy settle in you. When you open your eyes, you are back to being "you," but the cat is still within. Blow out the candle and sprinkle a few drops of beer or catnip tea about you, saying:

> *Great Goddess Bast!*
> *Black cat of joy and bliss*
> *Fill me forever*
> *With your happy kiss!*
> *Af An Nuteru Bast!*

Now clean up your things, get dressed up, go out, and cat around!

THE GODDESS Brigit

ORIGIN: Celtic
ATTRIBUTES: art, creativity, and inspiration
COLOR: white/red/black
SYMBOL: sun wheel (four-spoked wheel or cross) or anvil
ELEMENT: fire
STONE/METAL: garnet
SCENT: blackberry

Introduction

Drawn to the arts or crafts? Love anything creative and beautiful? Music, drama, or painting? If you are looking for a colorful and creative goddess, Brigit is the one! Call upon her for anything creative or artsy and she will inspire you!

Among the oldest and most worshipped of the Celtic goddesses is Brigit, whose cult may have extended over the entire empire of Brigantia, including parts of the British Isles as well as parts of Spain and France. She is patroness of poetry, arts, crafts, weaving, and inspiration. She is often divided into a triad with her two sisters, who govern smithcraft and medicine. Collectively they are known as the "three mothers" or the "three blessed ladies of Britain," and carvings of the three goddesses are common among the Celtic lands.

The Romans later identified her with Minerva, also a goddess of wisdom and handicrafts. Both also possess a warlike aspect, for Brigit's more active followers became known as brigands, from the old Irish *briga* or "warfare." The name Brigit appears to mean "bright one" or "bright arrow." At her temple in Kildare in Ireland, an eternal flame was guarded by a group of nineteen priestesses. This place later became a great convent famous for learning. Christians were not able to fully eradicate her worship and so were forced to canonize her as the famous Saint Bridget or Bride.

Sometimes she was declared to be the midwife of the Virgin Mary and the foster mother of Christ; often she was in fact identified with Mary herself. Her worship still survives in folk magick and popular belief. Her ancient festival on February 1, Oimelc or Imbolc, became the feast of the purification of the virgin, better known as Candlemas in the church calendar. This holiday is still recognized as one of the eight sabbats of the Wicca and the first day of spring by many.

Because of her many creative aspects and skills we call upon her for the spark of inspiration and creativity in all the arts.

* * * * *

*I*NVOCATION OF BRIGIT

Brigit! Brigit! Brigit!
Bright lady of the golden sun,
Queen of the poet's songs,
Triple mother of the emerald land
And teacher of many skills
Fill us with artistry and inspiration!

Your beauty inspires words of praise,
Your wisdom guides the world;
The bards of old were your followers
Who devoted their love to you!

At your altar burns eternal fire,
The secrets of your worship
Burn at the heart of the kingdom!
Fill us with artistry and inspiration

The smith at the forge does your bidding:
With hammer and anvil and steel
Beats out new creations of skillful craft
Advancing the science of man!

The potter, weaver, and poet
Create in your name
Reflecting your sunlike glory
As jewel to all who love beauty!

Wise you are in secret lore,
And inspiration's fire
Springs from you as a ray of sun
To transform all the world!

Creation burns in the heart that knows you,
In the hand that does your work;
The artist and the architect
Weave with the loom of your skill!

The people rise and advance in knowledge
Passed down from ancient times,
And new things come that you inspire
In the light of the new age dawning
Fill us with artistry and inspiration!

By the song of the poet on the wind,
By the fire of the blacksmith's forge,
By the wellspring of healing waters
May the whole world be reborn!

Bright arrow of the burning sun,
Guard the living earth!
Triple mother of the ancient land,

Fill the world with art and beauty
Fill us with artistry and inspiration!

Brigit! Brigit! Brigit!

Goddess Brigit Visualization Exercise

Within the center of the world
You coil in the womb,
Awaiting rebirth.
The three mothers gather around you,
Brigit in triple form.
She is come to remake you
In the body of the earth.
As poet she speaks:
Your flesh is weak,
Knowing age and death.
In the heart of earth's fire
You shall be reforged
As the diamond body of eternity.
As smith she takes you up,
And casts you on the fire
Of inspiration,
Melting your form
And purging the dross.
Dissolving what was,
Dismembering you,
Surrounding you with the primal transforming flame.
With her tongs she draws you forth
And places you on the anvil,
With her hammer she beats you
And shapes you,
Reforges your body anew
With a diamond heart
And silver bones
And golden flesh;

With muscles of gleaming steel
And organs of bronze,
With blood of liquid fire
And a mind of pure light.
Again she casts you on the fire
And heats you till you burn
Brighter than the sun.
The fires fill you with creativity!
As artist then
She draws you forth,
And casts you in her cauldron
Of living waters;
In the sudden chill
All is hidden by clouds of steam
As the metal of your being is cooled.
The waters fill you with power!
You are healed and made strong.
You are filled with creative visions!
She draws you forth from the cauldron
As from the womb of rebirth;
She speaks again:
In fire and water of magick
You have been tempered
As a blade of steel,
Reforged as a thing of beauty
To empower the earth.
Your body of flesh is memory;
You live in a diamond body of light.
Go forth and make art!

* * * * *

Grand Empowerment Ritual of Brigit: Becoming the Art of Arts

To become more creative in whatever we do in life, be it programming computers, designing dresses, or throwing pots, we must go to the source of all that is creative: the goddess herself. Becoming Brigit is the triple-tongued flame of inspiration itself. Dive in!

This rite is a celebration of the goddess and the artist that is you! The goal is to increase the positive energy of any creative undertaking. The focus here is on doing this through the natural energies of the planet and creating harmonious flows of natural energy in the form of creative works.

This rite is written with voices that represent the goddess's triple aspects: one with book as poet; one with fire and hammer as smith; and one who governs the cauldron and the feast as healer. Of course one person could do all three invocations.

You Will Need

◉ some spring water
◉ a silver cup or bowl
◉ a single white candle
◉ pen, pencil, and paper
◉ matches

The Ritual

Find a sacred place filled with creative things. Set the candle in the silver cup or bowl and say:

> I sing of Brigit,
> Elder goddess of all people
> Image of natural energy
> And great giver of gifts to the tribe;
> To her wisdom and magick
> I offer skill and song!

Light the candle, saying:

> In Her name
> I kindle flame!
> Let the fire of energy
> Which changes all things
> Shine upon us
> And transform us!

Pour the water into the cup or bowl, saying:

> *In Her name*
> *The waters flow!*
> *Let us drink of wisdom*
> *Which gives life,*
> *To heal us*
> *And the world!*
> *Let the three who are one be summoned*
> *To guard and guide this circle of power!*

Now summon the elements. Face in turn east, south, west, and north.

Say each time:

To the East:

> *By the sword of Nuada do I call*
> *The winds of the eastern gate!*
> *May my voice be heard*
> *In the air energies of the world;*
> *Bear witness to my rite!*

To the South:

> *By the spear of Lugh do I call*
> *The fire energies of the southern gate!*
> *May my vision be bright*
> *As the sun and the moon;*
> *Bear witness to my rite!*

To West:

> *By the cauldron of Daghdha do I call*
> *The water energies of the western gate!*
> *Let me taste enchantments of rebirth*
> *That the cauldron of wisdom holds!*
> *Bear witness to my rite!*

To the North:

> *By the stone of Fal do I call*
> *The living earth energies of the northern gate!*
> *Throne of the kingdom*

> *And flesh of the queen,*
> *Bear witness to my rite!*

Stand, arms raised as the goddess, saying:
> *At the center where heaven and earth are one,*
> *At the center where fire and water mingle,*
> *Where spirit and nature touch,*
> *I stand and call the triple mothers*
> *The natural energies of the Earthspirit*
> *Brigit! Brigit! Brigit!*

Sprinkle some of the extra water and sip a little. Feel the energies of Brigit gather, and say:
> *Of old the people were gathered*
> *In the place where poets sang,*
> *The bards in holy madness*
> *Gave voice to my dreams!*
> *The energies art and creativity*
> *Fill me!*
> *Let all now come forward*
> *And let all voices rise*
> *And sing of the great goddess,*
> *She of ten thousand names!*
> *Art and beauty!*

Now, you must write the final call to her with a poem written by you. Begin with:
> *I am the bright one!*
> *I am the triple flame of the sun!*
> *I am art and beauty and inspiration!*
> *I am the goddess of infinite forms!*

Continue your poem from there. End with:
> *I am Brigit*
> *I am Brigid*
> *I am Bride*
> *The eternally creative:*
> *May all do art*

And live in beauty!
And so I go out *to do my art*
As a golden arrow shot
From the sun.

Dana Brigid!

Meditate. Create with the objects you brought. Be open to art.

When you come back to yourself, sprinkle some of the water to the four directions and the center and say:

I have come to sing of Brigit,
Elder goddess of my people,
Great giver of gifts to the tribe;
Mother of natural earth energies
To her wisdom and magick
We have offered our skill and song and art!
The fire has warmed me,
The water has cooled me,
The wind bore my words
To the four corners of the earth!
I now go in peace,
To make art in the world!
Hail Brigit! May the light rise about us!

Blow out the candle, and bury it and the water in the earth.

Drink from the same bowl or cup whenever you need artistic inspiration!

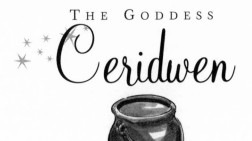

THE GODDESS
Ceridwen

ORIGIN: Wales
ATTRIBUTE: inspiration, knowledge, and deep things
COLOR: dark green
SYMBOL: cauldron
ELEMENT: water
STONE/METAL: bronze
SCENT: yarrow or willow tree

INTRODUCTION

Want inner knowledge, wisdom, and to really be able to uncover secrets and hidden information? Invoke the great mother of all deep knowledge, Ceridwen.

The great Goddess Ceridwen is a Welsh mother, a mistress of magick, and a giver of wisdom. Her symbol is the cauldron of inspiration and rejuvenation common in many of the ancient Celtic mythologies, as a vessel of transformation on many levels.

The cauldron may be seen as a source of food, a cornucopia of inexhaustible plenty. It is the vessel used to brew the drink of inspiration and poetry, whether mead, beer, or wine, and it is the source of holy ecstasy and intoxication. It may restore the dead to life. In later times it became the tool of witches and wisewomen, where herbal cures and strange potions seethed. The cauldron on the cooking-hearth is one of the oldest technologies and symbols of wealth and plenty in human history. In medieval and Renaissance times, subsumed into the Arthurian tales, it becomes indistinguishable from the Holy Grail.

Ceridwen's name means "white sow," which links her to many other primordial goddesses with sow aspects (such as Demeter and Freya); she is also linked to the moon. A great sorceress and poet, she is said to have had two children with her husband, Tegid foel. She had a beautiful daughter named Creirwy, and an extremely ugly and misshapen son called Afagddu ("utter darkness") or Morfran ("great crow"). While little else is known about her family, she prepared a brew in her cauldron of inspiration, simmering magickal herbs for the cycle of a full year to gift her son with some talents in life. She set an old blind man to stir it, and a young boy named Gwion to fetch wood. At the end of the year, three drops leaped out of the cauldron and splashed on this child servant of hers, and when he put his burned finger in his mouth he received the full benefit of the spell. It enraged her that he received the magical blessing that was to be her son's.

Fleeing her wrath, he changed into many forms, while she herself pursued him, changing into even more dangerous forms in turn. He was hare and she was hound; then fish and otter, bird and hawk. At last he became a grain of wheat and hid among the harvest, and she as a white hen searched him out. Eventually Ceridwen captured and devoured him. Nine months later he was reborn to her as Taliesin, among the most famous of Celtic prophets and poets. This myth is the basis of the grand ritual in this section. As Ceridwen is a lady of the moon, we have called her as a transformer of elements by magickal means. We invoke her for wisdom, for knowing the inner truths of ourselves and others, and for deep visionary knowledge.

* * * * *

INVOCATION OF CERIDWEN

In the darkness of night,
In the wilderness of time,

By the ancient name we invoke thee:
Ceridwen! Ceridwen! Ceridwen!

Lady of the triple moon,
Maiden, mother, and wise crone,
Ever changing and unchanging,
Mystery of life becoming.

By the winds about the world,
Ever whirling in their course,
Shared as the breath of every life
Which speaks all words of power!

By the waters of wine-dark sea,
Waves that shake the solid land,
Ocean womb which brings forth life
To rise and grow and change!

By the fires of transformation
That blaze and burn,
That spiral and turn,
That fill the darkness with shadow!

By the stone beneath our feet,
By the sky above our heads,
By the birds and beasts and fish
Which teem with life about us!

In the darkness of night,
In the wilderness of time,
By the ancient name we invoke thee:
Ceridwen! Ceridwen! Ceridwen!

By the cauldron of wisdom
And transformation,
Where seethes the brew
Of inspiration.

Stirring the mead of poetry
In the songs of all hearts,

Bringing the miracle unceasing
To the work of all hands!

In the womb of the goddess
Where magick finds birth
And the secret is held
For the healing of earth,

We find the sacred mystery
As the triple moon turns,
We transform ourselves
Where the bright fire burns!

When the spell is spoken
Our will is done,
As the call goes forth
We summon your love:

In the darkness of night,
In the wilderness of time,
By the ancient name we invoke thee:
Ceridwen! Ceridwen! Ceridwen!

The storm clouds fly
From the moon's fair face,
The whirling winds
Turn the tides of the deep.

The silver mirror reflects the void,
Dreams are born into flesh;
Out of the silence new songs are sung,
New prophecies are made.

We drink the brew
Of the poet's knowing,
Burn with the fire
Of magick growing.

We dance the turning
Of the silver wheel,

Build the castle of glass
By the wave-swept shore.

In the darkness of night,
In the wilderness of time,
By the ancient name we invoke thee:
Ceridwen! Ceridwen! Ceridwen!

* * * * *

GODDESS CERIDWEN VISUALIZATION EXERCISE

See that the green is the sea herself.
You float in the heart of the ocean,
Wrapped in the dream of the deep.
You drift in the warm gulf currents,
Carried gently over the darker icy deeps,
Sensing the waving weeds as you pass
Over the shallows where the sunlight dances.
The schools of fish flash around you,
Dancing swift with feather touch;
The songs of the whales, deep and sonorous,
Resonate through your bones
Shaking you with their ancient tones.
Pulled by the tides, this way and that,
You grow tenuous and diffused,
Spread wider and thinner through waters,
Made one with their ebb and flow.
You are the sea,
From surface to silent depths of the trench
Beyond all reach of earthly life.
Frozen at the poles you are,
And warm as blood at the equator,
Touched by every river and stream
That flow down from the high mountains.
You are the sea,
The great lakes and the oceans,
Whose arms embrace island and archipelago,

Whose hands grasp the beaches with pounding surf.
A universe unto yourself, you drift and dream
In the songs of the tide, the dance of the moon.

Further and further away you drift
From everything that you once were;
Humanity seems remote from the liquid realm
That you now inhabit wholly.
Memory of earthly life is distant,
Nothing remains that is solid.
Turning and coiling, you dissolve,
Becoming ethereal, rising upward,
Drawn still by the silver touch of moon glow
Which reaches down from the heavens to touch you,
Caress you, lure you higher.
Waters become misty vapors,
Fog drifting on the face of the deep;
Wind currents take the place of tides.
In whirling eddies you lose all shape,
Grow more tenuous, fainter of form.
Caught in the breeze you rise,
The spiraling vortex ascending
On atmospheric currents;
In cloud form you wander aimless,
Drawn by the whims of air.
Rising still, you reach toward upper reaches
Where only eagles soar alone;
You spread yourself wide
On the very edge of open space,
Coiling about the globe like a serpent
Wrapped about her egg.
Silence now, in the face of the stillness of night;
Solitude, beyond the reach of gravity.
It is pure here,
This is the place of true wisdom
True knowledge

Inner knowing
And nothing intercedes between you
And the silver mask that hides the lady's face
In changing moods that wax and wane.
The gaze of the goddess is upon you,
Her eyes all-knowing in wisdom of love
And experience of all the ages.
This is the moon that looked upon primal earth
And saw all life evolve in waves;
The eras of fire and ice,
Of parching drought and advancing glacier,
Conquering in their turn,
The drifting of continents and the rise of mountains,
The slow change from forest to desert.
All she sees and all she knows,
Caught up in the endless cycle of play
Guided by her soft-sung spells;
The changing moon, the lunar queen,
She who rules heaven and earth
And the fortunes of men and women.
You are bathed in her silver light,
In the silence at the edge of space,
Until the solitude of communion with her power
And you have new knowledge
And you are filled with wisdom
And you know the deep mysteries!
Then you turn inward, coiling about yourself,
And fall slowly back to the core of your being,
The form of your body
That comes to rest at the very center of the earth;
You descend into manifestation
And take up the burden of flesh once more;
You rest, breathing deeply,
Waking slowly as from sleep.

Goddess Empowerment Ritual of Ceridwen — Rite of the Inner Knowing: The Cauldron of Transformation

The purpose of this ritual is to become the goddess of all understanding and thus gain inner knowing and wisdom. Isn't that great? We all could be a bit wiser!

Its form is reminiscent of the primal shamanic circle dance, or perhaps the classic witch's sabbat experience.

You Will Need

◎ a large cauldron (or cooking pot) with boiling spring water

◎ flowers and herbs to be thrown in the "cauldron" —
sage, mint, rosemary, bay leaf, and thyme are
all excellent. You may add any others you wish, especially
herbs that represent wisdom or mental clarity!

◎ matches

◎ three blue candles

◎ teacup

The Ritual

In the course of this rite you will dance around the pot, imitating the forms of the various animal spirits of the world: red-blooded beasts for fire; fish for water; and birds for the air, with seeds for the earth. As the power is raised for each of these realms it is concentrated into the cauldron swirling with all evolutionary energies, the great unconscious mind!

The goal here is for the ritualists to act out the primal myth of Ceridwen, one of transformation and initiation. The ideal site for this would be a beach, as the seashore represents a symbolic boundary place between the worlds. For the landlocked, any large body of water would suffice; if absolutely necessary an indoor situation is okay. Just place the pot (on a plate) and pour boiling water into the pot just before the rite, or use a small hotplate.

To begin, fill the cauldron (pot) with pure water and light the fire underneath or pour boiling water carefully into the "cauldron" in the middle of your sacred place. Place the flowers about it and light the three candles.

After meditating on Ceridwen and her myths (see the introduction of this chapter) begin to stare into the cauldron and think about the meaning of wisdom and knowledge, saying:

> *I come to call on Ceridwen,*
> *Triple goddess of the moon,*
> *Muse of song and sorceress,*
> *Maiden, mother, and crone.*
> *By the cauldron where magick is brewed*
> *And the secrets of change are born*
> *I conjure new transformations*
> *Of the lives upon the earth.*
> *Heal the earth! Rebirth!*

Now call to the four corners, saying:

To the East:

> *Winds of life we call to change,*
> *Bring me wisdom and inner knowledge!*
> *May I be born again to brightness!*
> *May the air be reborn!*

To the South:

> *Fires burning in our houses*
> *Set free the souls of hidden knowing;*
> *Bring me wisdom and inner knowledge!*
> *Find wisdom's liberation!*
> *May the flames be reborn!*

To the West:

> *Waters churning with understanding,*
> *Grow clean and clear and pure with knowing*
> *Bring me wisdom and inner knowledge*
> *To give new life to all.*
> *May the oceans be reborn!*

To the North:

> *Deep earth, hidden understanding*

Grow green again as once before
Bring me wisdom and inner knowledge!
Return me to the primal knowing!
May the world be reborn!

Now you will become the shadow goddess of knowing yourself!

Read the following while circling the steaming "cauldron" and casting herbs into the brew:

I am the elder power of change,
The mystery of transformation.
In my cauldron I brew the healing of the world,
The resurrection of wind and wave
Let the earth be made full of wisdom!
Let the winds be full of wisdom!
Let the waters flow full of wisdom!
By the power of the magickal fire
I weave the spell to return again to the world of ancient times
The world of ancient times, full of wisdom!
When grass grew green
And the waves were blue,
The clouds white as snow.
Return the dream of the time of beginnings,
When all knew their true names
I am Ceridwen!
I know all names and truths!
So mote it be!

Squat and deeply breathe in the steam. Feel the cloak of supreme wisdom settle on you. Open the inner eye. Remember, you are the goddess of deep understanding!

But the wisdom flees you as a small boy flees the goddess. You must catch the wisdom to become it all! Say:

Where is the wisdom of the world?
It has been taken!
Flee me now, though I pursue,
In changing shapes of hunting!

Now, slowly circle the cauldron, changing shapes in your mind as you chant the following:

> Wisdom has fled as a hare, over rough ground,
> Running swift beneath trees, lit by the moon,
>
> I have followed as a greyhound swift,
> Sharp of tooth and keen to track;
>
> The fire of your blood in the chase will not hide you,
> For your greed has made you blind!
> Run for your life, my foolish child,
> For I shall have you
> And then will come knowledge!
>
> Wisdom has fled as a fish, a salmon of silver,
> Scaled with rainbows of light;
>
> I have followed as an otter seeking,
> Rough of pelt, with grasping claw;
>
> The waters green will cast you out,
> For your greed has made you blind!
> Run for your life, my foolish child,
> For I shall have you
> And then will come knowledge!
>
> Wisdom has fled as a songbird, brightly feathered,
> Who rides the winds and nests in the tree limbs.
>
> I have followed as a hawk, eyes as keen as the sun;
> With beak and claw I strike and tear,
>
> The wind in the trees will help you not,
> For your greed has made you blind!
> Run for your life, my foolish child,
> For I shall have you
> And then will come knowledge!
>
> Wisdom falls to the earth as a seed of grain,
> It hides in the field of harvest;

> *I become a white hen, who scratches and seeks,*
> *Whose appetite is endless!*
>
> *The earth herself will not hide you,*
> *For your greed has made you blind!*
> *Run for your life, my foolish child,*
> *For I shall have you*
> *And then will come knowledge!*

Finally, as the goddess, fall to the earth with your face covered.

The goddess touches you then. Find the wisdom you have hunted in the darkness, join with Ceridwen! Then carefully dip the teacup in the brew and take three sips. You now have the wisdom.

Rise and say:

> *I have passed the ordeals*
> *And am born to wisdom;*
> *I have drunk deep of magick*
> *And been transformed!*
> *I gather my inner knowing in this circle,*
> *And work for deep understanding*
> *By the blessing of Ceridwen!*

Sprinkle some of the brew to the four directions while saying:

> *Well and wisely the spell is cast,*
> *Long may the power raised here last!*
> *Let the cauldron now be poured*
> *Over the stones of all the Earth!*
> *Let the force of the fire*
> *Be one with the world!*
> *Heal the Earth—rebirth!*

Blow out the candles and be silent, then go.

The brew can be strained and saved for other rites or shared with friends in need of wisdom. The rest of the brew, herbs, and flowers should all be tossed into water of some kind.

THE GODDESS Demeter

ORIGIN: Greek
ATTRIBUTES: motherhood and nurturing
COLOR: tan/gold
SYMBOL: sheaf of wheat
ELEMENT: earth
STONE/METAL: geode
SCENT: grass, oils from seeds

INTRODUCTION

Everyone needs Mom sometimes, just as everyone is Mom to somebody sometimes. When we need nurturing, and TLC, only Mom can really give us what we need. Well, Demeter is Mom with a capital *M*. If you need mothering or need to give mothering, nurturing, and unconditional love, call on her. You can never go wrong with Mom!

The great Goddess Demeter is counted among the gods of Olympus, but may well be far older in origin. Some scholars say she is the primal earth mother of ancient times, and she is indeed also the corn mother and the grain goddess, who "fed" humanity. It is she who causes the crops to grow; she who brings life to the fields.

Demeter is said to be wed to Poseidon, the god of the sea who embraces the land. Their daughter is Kore the Maiden, also called Perse-phone, queen of the land of the dead. Their story forms the mythic origin of the Mysteries of Eleusis, one of the greatest unifying religious move-ments of the Greeks.

One day, it was told, Persephone was picking flowers with her young companions when Hades, ruler of the underworld (the third brother of Zeus and Poseidon, who controlled the sky and the sea respectively), beheld her and fell deeply in love. Rising from a cavern in his great chariot drawn by black horses, he seized Persephone and carried her away to the land of the dead. Demeter, torn by grief at the mysterious loss of her daughter, wandered the world in search of her. While she did so no seed would sprout, no crop would grow, no life was born, and the human race was in great danger of extinction. In time, she disguised herself and traveled to the kingdom of Eleu-sis, where she became the nurse of the royal family's children. Eventually her true identity was revealed and she was again worshipped as a goddess in their temple. Seeing her there, and fearing for the future of the human race, the deities of Olympus sent their messenger Hermes to ask her to allow the crops to grow again, but she refused to do so until her daughter was returned to her.

Zeus, the king of the gods, sent for his brother Hades to ask for Perse-phone's return, and Hades agreed to do so on condition that Persephone spend most of the year in the land of the living and return to the land of the dead in the winter. Thus she became both the honored queen of the underworld and the personification of the spring, and the stored or buried seed that rises to new life.

Joyously reunited with her daughter, Demeter allowed the earth to return to fertility and taught the people of Eleusis the secrets of agricul-ture. This city became one of the major centers of her Mysteries. The reuniting of mother and daughter, and the yearly renewal of the fields that gave life, were cause for great festival and celebration.

Demeter is not just a goddess of food, nurturing, and fertility, she rep-resents the very power and essence of motherhood and the pure love of a parent for her child. This love is the highest vibration of energy in the uni-verse. Call upon her and become this pure love!

The offerings appropriate to Demeter are fresh fruits of the earth: grapes rather than wine, grain rather than bread, honey not mead; flowers of all kinds, but most especially the poppy. Her image is of a queen enthroned, giving an ear of corn or sheaf of wheat. She is the grain mother, the friend of farmers, who pours out the fruits of the earth to feed her children. Her candles should be yellow, the color of corn or wheat.

* * * * *

INVOCATION OF DEMETER

Great one, hear me now!
Demeter! Demeter! Demeter!
Corn mother,
Grain goddess,
Giver of life to the land,
We call you!
Despoena
Daeira
Heiros Pluto!

Ancient one,
Beautiful and mysterious,
Enthroned in secret,
Mother of wisdom of the earth,
I call you!

Mother of the maiden Kore,
Searcher for the lost one,
Full of love
Wanderer over the wide world
Who brings back life to the fields,
I call you!

Earth-bride of the sea king,
Ever-fertile life giver,
By the field that is plowed
And the seed that is sown,
I call you!

By the growing grain
And the harvest scythe,
By the sprouting seed
That gives new life,
Nurturer!
I call you!

Mother of the farmlands
Who blesses herds and flocks,
Who watches over families
And always cares for children,
I call you!

Great mother of humanity,
Reveal the mysteries of new growth,
Rejuvenate my soul
Teach the ways of compassion and love
To the folk of every land!
I call you!

We are your children;
Give us your mother's love!
We remember your name when men forget truth,
We sing your praise and give thanks!
I call you!

Clear-eyed Demeter,
Serene of brow and beautiful,
Hair golden as ripening grain,
Great queen crowned with corn,
Ma!
I call you!

By the harvest sheaf
And the future's seed,
By the fiery torch
Of summer's sunlight,
I call you!

By the temples of stone now fallen,
By the love in your worshipper's hearts,
By the healing milk of the mother's breast
And the secrets of new creation,
I call you!

Demeter! Demeter! Demeter!
Corn mother
Grain goddess
Despoena
Daeira
Heiros Pluto!
One who always loves
We call you!

* * * * *

GODDESS DEMETER VISUALIZATION EXERCISE

At first there is nothing
But the glow of warm green light
Which surrounds you with a feeling
Of total security.
Like a child in her mother's embrace.
Slowly the light grows brighter,
Ever more golden,
Until it seems as though
You are at the very heart of the sun,
The seething core of solar fire.
You feel the weight of immense gravity,
The density of unspeakable mass,
The solidity of ultimate stone
Filling your body with massive power.
You realize then that this is not the sun,
But the earth herself,
At whose core of molten stone
Lies the still center of the spinning globe,

The heart of all her life.
Through her body of living rock
The liquid lava flows like blood
To warm the skin of her surface
Which swarms and teems
With birds, beasts, and fish;
With fields and forests
Moved by the warm wind.
The goddess is robed with the
Ever-changing colors of the sea,
Which dance and turn about her form
In shades of blue, green, and gray.
Here and there she is jeweled
With the lights of the cities
And the bands of roadways,
The ceaseless motion
And thought of humanity,
Creating and destroying endlessly.
This multitude of lives
Is one great life,
The profusion of souls
One solitary soul,
Dancing to the rhythm of a single beating heart.
The sphere spins in its orbital dance,
Whirling through endless days and nights
And the slower pace of changing seasons,
Ever returning to the place of beginning.

Rising above into darkness of space,
You see the world as a wheel,
As a jewel of brightness spinning,
A circle of endless miracles.
From the distance of high orbit
You begin to see the presence
Whose body encompasses the globe
As the fullness within her womb,

The child of ever-becoming life.
She is the mother of all,
The queen of joy and compassion
Who gives and takes all.
Her hand upholds the ways of humanity,
Her eye lies behind all seeing,
Her mind behind all knowing.
She sees your innermost heart
And draws you higher
To your ultimate destiny.
She is all-loving.
In the light of her gaze
You are filled with fire,
Glowing and golden,
Fading back into green,
As you fall away from the vision;
Back to the earth,
Back to your body,
Knowing you are loved deeply,
Knowing that the great mother cares about you
Feeling warm and protected and nurtured
By the mother of all
Demeter rocks you with love
You breathe in silence for a time
Then return to the world
Still feeling her embrace.

* * * * *

GRAND EMPOWERMENT RITUAL OF DEMETER: THE NURTURING OF ALL

Gather food and prepare a great feast. Some of what you gather may be given to friends, loved ones, family, or whoever needs nurturing and care. To become Demeter is to become a giver, a nurturer, a loving mother to all.

If you can, do this ritual in a suitable and powerful site on local farmland or food garden. If you have to be inside, choose a maternal or comforting room and fill it with nurturing and mother-love items.

You Will Need

◎ a small drum
◎ an image of the Goddess Demeter
◎ some water in a large pitcher
◎ a handful of dried corn kernels
◎ matches
◎ two candles, one green and one yellow
◎ frankincense incense
◎ a bottle of whole milk
◎ a woven basket holding a clay cup
◎ yellow flowers (sunflowers are perfect)
◎ a spade or trowel
◎ bread, pears, apples, grapes, and cheese

The Ritual

Proceed to the site in a slow procession, tapping the drum in good spirits. Establish an altar of beauty on a stone, then place the image or symbol of Demeter in the center and sit in silence.

When ready, pour a little water over your hands, saying:

Let the waters of life and memory
Wash me clean of the dust of the mundane
That I may come to speak with the goddess
In a sacred place of purity and peace.
Kyria!

Toss a few corn kernels to the four directions, then sprinkle some in a clockwise circle about you, saying:

Heiros heiros heiros!
I come here to worship Demeter,
Great corn mother of all living,
Guardian of the wide fields of grain
And generous giver of the fruits of the earth.
I call her now as a child
Call with longing to her mother!

Nurture me, comfort me, fill me
With your endless and overflowing love!
Kyria Demeter!

Light the candles and incense on the stone altar and say:
Grain mother, bread giver,
Great Demeter, we call you!
By the sun's golden light
And the scent of summer flowers;
By the fields of wheat and corn and rye,
By the seeds that ever give new life
Nurture me, comfort me, fill me
With your endless and overflowing love!
Kyria Demeter!

At each of the four directions, read the appropriate verse with your arms raised:
I call upon Euros,
The wind of the East,
To witness this rite.
May the grain grow tall
In the fields of earth
And love fill every heart!

I call upon Notos,
The wind of the South,
To witness this rite.
May the grain grow tall
In the fields of earth
And love fill every heart!

I call upon Zephyros,
The wind of the West,
To witness this rite.
May the grain grow tall
In the fields of earth
And love fill every heart!

> I call upon Boreas,
> The wind of the North,
> To witness this rite.
> May the grain grow tall
> In the fields of earth
> And love fill every heart!

Sprinkle the last of the corn in a circle around the food. Bless the food offering, saying:

> Here is the place of plenty
> Where the waving grain grows
> In the love of every heart.
> The love of the mother!
> Gold of grain and wealth of crops,
> Golden sun and wealth of nations,
> Hearts of compassion and caring united
> I call on the great goddess
> To pour out food for the starving,
> Drink for those athirst,
> That the children of earth may grow strong,
> And the world be healed of sorrow
> Fill me, O Mother
> With thy love and prosperity
> Let it flow through me
> Kyria Demeter!

Open the milk, hold it aloft, and say:

> Great Demeter,
> Eternal Earth embraced by the sea,
> Giver of life to all!
> Remember the children of the world!
> Remember me, who you gave birth to!
> By your ever-flowing breasts
> I offer you milk, O Mother,
> I burn incense to your name!
> By full fields and fine orchards
> And gardens of richness

> *May the earth grow strong*
> *For the generations to come*
> *May your love flow into and through me*
> *Heiros!*

Take a big drink of the milk from the clay cup, pour a little on the earth as offering, and feel the power and golden glow of the great mother fill you with the most primal love! Pick up the drum and begin to sway and play while chanting:

> *Kyria Demeter: Grain grow above!*
> *Kyria Demeter: Fill me with love!*
> *Kyria Demeter: Grain grow above!*
> *Kyria Demeter: Fill me with love!*
> *Kyria Demeter: Grain grow above!*
> *Kyria Demeter: Fill me with love!*

Visualize an ever-widening circle of light spreading from your glowing being at the center of the circle, expanding to cover the globe. Then sit in silence and meditation for a time on *being* love, *being* nurturing, *being* the mother of the world. When you are the golden mother, stand holding the flowers and the ear of corn, saying:

> *I am Demeter!*
> *Queen with crown*
> *Of flowers bright,*
> *Whose scepter is*
> *A sheaf of grain;*
>
> *Queen whose dance*
> *Is season's change*
> *Of growing green*
> *And falling rain;*
>
> *I am lady bright who*
> *Sows and reaps,*
> *Brings the harvest*
> *Grain all gold;*
>
> *I teach the making*
> *Of bread and beer,*

Of loving and birthing
In the turning
Of the year.

From the seed
To sprouting shoot,
By the leaf
Of flower and fruit;

By the new seed
Come again,
And the cycle
Of new grain,

Guard the garden
And the field,
Hallow all the
Crops shall yield.

From summer sun
To winter rest,
Sowing spring
Through fall harvest,

I bless orchard trees
And flowers here,
The healing herbs
Of every year.

I am queen with crown
Of flowers bright,
Whose scepter is
A sheaf of grain;

Queen whose dance
Is season's change
Of growing green
And falling rain!

I am Mother Demeter
I hold every child
Kind to every animal
Nurturing and supporting
To all who need it!

Io evoe!
I am Demeter!
Io evoe!
I am the love of the mother!
My heart fills the world
All becomes gold
In my sheltering arms!
Kyria! Heiros! Io evoe!

Meditate long and enjoy the wonders of being the eternal loving mother force.

When you "come back" to the mundane world and return to being you, close the ritual by eating some of the food and saying:

I give thanks to the great Goddess Demeter,
Who gives plenty to the fields and crops
Love and support to all men and women
And guards the community
Of all living things!
We make offerings in return
To she who gives us all nourishment!

Pour out the rest of the milk into a hole dug in the earth with the spade or trowel.

May we all be fed
And no child go hungry
May we all receive the love and care
We need and deserve
We give thanks to the great mother of life,
And to the four winds which guard us.

Turn to the four directions and say in turn:

Euros, wind of the East,
Spread the seed of golden love
For the healing of the earth!
We thank you!

Notos, wind of the South,
Spread the seed of golden love
For the healing of the earth!
We thank you!

Zephyros, wind of the West,
Spread the seed of golden love
For the healing of the earth!
We thank you!

Boreas, wind of the North,
Spread the seed of golden love
For the healing of the earth!
We thank you!

Now exit in a solemn manner, leaving the site clean and clear. Carry off the food in the basket to give to others, saying:

Heal the earth, with love, rebirth!
Heal the earth, with love, rebirth!
Heal the earth, with love, rebirth!

Go love and be loved.

THE GODDESS Fortuna

ORIGIN: Roman
ATTRIBUTE: good luck
COLOR: gold
SYMBOL: wheel of fortune
ELEMENT: Earth
STONE/METAL: all jewels or diamonds
SCENT: poppy

INTRODUCTION

She is the triple goddess of fate. Fortuna can be seen as the unknown power of all coincidence and synchronicity or even karma. She is the mysterious mind of the universe that somehow decides the fortunes of all humanity. From the dawn of time humans have sought to influence the apparent whims of reality that surround us; magick, religion, and science have all taken their turn. Need to get lucky? Need some good fortune to enter your life? Feel jinxed and want the universe to smile on you again? Call upon the Goddess Fortuna, Lady Luck!

The power of fate personified is this goddess. She was Fortuna to the Romans. Her name may be derived from *Vortumna*, which means "she who turns the year."

While many aspects of the goddess appear universal and thus impersonal, it seems that Fortuna was in some ways recognized as having a more intimate connection with human beings. It was believed that everyone had his own spirit of luck to guide him through life, like a guardian angel.

Among the titles associated with this goddess are Fortuna Primigeneia, the firstborn; Fortuna Muliebris, goddess of women; Fortuna Scribunda, the fate who writes; and Bona Fortuna or Mala Fortuna, good and bad fate. She was also known as Fortuna Augusti or Fortuna Regia, meaning personification of the emperor's rulership. A golden statue of her accompanied the emperors at all times and was passed along to their successors.

Fortuna's symbol is a wheel. In ancient times, on calendar wheels, even numbers were male, and odd numbers, female; odd-numbered days were considered more favorable for festivals. This distinction survives today on roulette wheels. Red is for female, black is male.

The ever-popular roulette wheel indicates the element of chance and of pleasure inherent in life, however much of a gamble it may seem. It should be noted that early games were often teaching tools as well as instruments for determining the fates or the will of the gods.

Fortuna is the goddess who personifies the power of the universe as fortune or, some would say, karma. Fortuna reminds us that we are not separate from the natural cycles, but are a very important part of the cycles of life. She reminds us that every action we take on the planet has many effects that last a long time. Thus we invoke her to help us understand these cycles, gain good fortune, and to help the fortunes of others.

* * * * *

ℐNVOCATION OF THE GODDESS FORTUNA

Wise Fortuna,
Lady of fate,
Perfection of paradox
I call you!
Golden image of our desire,
Fleeting form that lures us onward,

Wind of change that shakes the world,
Turning wheel of rise and fall
And destiny unknowable;
Fire in the core of my being
And rainbow dancer manifesting miracles;
Bona Fortuna, I call you
Bring me good fortune
Bring me luck!
May I command the wheel of life!

Fortuna Augusti,
Who governs the nations
And all of humanity's fates;
Great mystery
Of the turning wheel,
The twist and turn
Of all time and tide.
I call you by the names of old,
You who raise empires and cause them to fall,
Who measures the music
Of the everlasting dance.
Bring me good fortune
Bring me luck!
May I command the wheel of life!

At the gate of the North
By the strength of stone
I invoke your law:
Fortuna Primigenia,
Firstborn goddess,
Who opened the gates of beginning;
Who walked in the dreamtime of creation,
And gives the true names
That cause life to have form
Make me aware of the cycle of life!
Bring me good fortune

Bring me luck!
May I command the wheel of life!

At the gate of the East
By the wings of the wind
I invoke your life:
Fortuna Scribunda,
Who writes the fates,
Spins, measures, and cuts the threads of lives.
You carve the runes on the tree of worlds,
You sing the songs in the sacred language,
Record all the words that are spoken
Teach us the wisdom of the cycle of life!
Bring me good fortune
Bring me luck!
May I command the wheel of life!

At the gate of the South
By the flowering fire
I invoke your light:
Fortuna Regia,
Giver of royalty,
Who makes queens and kings
Out of women and men,
Who crowns with silver and gold
All those who live their true will.
Bring me good fortune
Bring me luck!
May I command the wheel of life!

At the gate of the West
Where the waters flow
I invoke your love:
Fortuna Muliebris,
Goddess of women,
Who walks the earth in a multitude of forms
And guides the generations

Through all cycles of time,
Through the millions of years to eternity.
Bring me good fortune
Bring me luck!
May I command the wheel of life!

In the sacred center of the wheel,
The omphallos stands as the navel of earth,
Mark of the cord that links us
To the universal womb wherein we grow.
By the triple norns and moraie,
The weavers at the well,
The spinners of the wheel of change
And the cycle of life and death and life,
I invoke you!
Make me see the whole of life!
Bring me good fortune
Bring me luck!
May I command the wheel of life!

Bona Fortuna,
Look favorably upon us!
Mala Fortuna,
Avert your gaze!
May the fates be kind
And lady luck smile!

By the great mandala of creation
And the changing pattern
Of the everlasting dance,
May the work bear fruit
Unto countless generations.
Wise Fortuna,
Lady of fate,
Perfection of paradox,
We thank you!
Bring me good fortune

Bring me luck!
May I command the wheel of life!
Salve Fortuna!

Goddess Fortuna Visualization Exercise

All around you is spinning color,
Like rainbows gone mad
Or a whirlpool of light,
A field of forces that pulls on your limbs,
Whips through your hair
Like the wild windstorm.
You feel it to the center of your being,
A centrifugal current that shakes your bones,
Vibrates through you
Like the earthquake or the tidal wave.
You shake in the grip of the gods.
Out of the chaos order is born;
Visions flow of history,
The movement of peoples
And the rise and fall of nations,
The voyages of explorers
And the lives of families,
The rhythms of cities
And the peace of small villages,
The movement on roadways
And the dreams of slumber.
In the eye of your mind they dwell:
The works and follies,
Fortunes and losses,
Joys and sorrows of humanity.
Behind this mask of constant change
You glimpse a visage serene and calm
Who touches all with unseen hands
And turns this wheel of fortune.

She is hard to focus upon,
Impossible to define;
Reach out to her and she cannot be touched,
Listen to the errant strains of her music
Which drift like colors on the breeze
As they slip away again.
She is beyond and behind the senses;
She is more a part of you than blood or bone
And yet you cannot grasp her.
Golden and mercurial,
Swifter than sight of the eye,
She dances, whirling ceaselessly
As the world spins and the planets turn
And the stars weave patterns of fate.
She is the trickster
Who builds up and tears down cultures,
Fools people into wisdom,
Tricks them into truth.
She dances, and all follow her rhythm
Of rise and fall in turn;
She is the first cause of all creation,
The mother of miracle and catastrophe,
Of terrible accidents and happy coincidences,
Of discovery and loss, of lies and truth.
Never where you think she is
And found where you least expect her,
She delights and surprises,
Disappoints and dismays,
Reveals and conceals all mysteries.
Earthquake and whirlwind, fire and flood
Follow in her footsteps;
Blessing and healing and inspiration
Are poured from her hands.
Nothing but paradox may describe her,
Contradiction and change are her constant qualities.
She gazes upon you and blesses you

Good fortune fills you!
She moves in mysterious ways,
And you cannot guess
Which way
She will turn next.

* * * * *

GRAND EMPOWERMENT RITUAL OF FORTUNA: BECOMING THE WHEEL OF THE LIVING WORLD, THE POWER OF GOOD FORTUNE

Become Fortuna if you are in need of a change of luck, or wish to turn the wheel and bring good things into your life. This empowerment is particularly good for invoking good fortune or ensuring the fortune of another person, group, or project.

You Will Need

◉ salt
◉ a wheel or image of one
◉ coins
◉ matches
◉ flowery incense, such as rose or jasmine
◉ a golden cup of wine
◉ fruit and flowers as you like
◉ three gold candles
◉ an image of the goddess
◉ a lucky charm and gold or yellow clothing to wear

The Ritual

Set up your sacred place outside on top of a hill or cliff or inside. Try to get up as high as possible.

Sprinkle salt about the circle first to banish any bad luck!

When ready, meditate on all the aspects of fortune and karma, touch the wheel of Fortuna symbol you have on the altar and say:

The world spins
I come here

So that proper order
May be restored
And balance
And good fortune
Be manifest!
I speak for spirit,
Born of infinite space
In union with eternity.
How shall we bring fortune
To the world of matter?

Touch the coins, saying:
I speak for the earth.
We are born and die
On this one planet,
Prospering and losing
I must restore my center
As followers of the lady did of old:
The circle
The life of the circle
The touch of these coins
How we chose to live our lives
The balance of karma
Here is the true center of our lives.

Light the incense, and say:
I speak for the air:
The winds that whirled
At the dawn of time
Sometimes blowing where
We did not wish to go
In place of this,
I offer here
Sweet-smelling offerings
Of Fortuna's breath
And the thoughts of winds
Bringing good fortune!

Sprinkle a little wine on the flowers and say:

I speak for water!
The oceans are
Our planet's womb;
All life evolved
In the tidal seas.
We began our climb
In the depths,
We live and prosper
In the depths of our minds and souls.
All share our common ancestry
We are all part of the wheel
I call you, Fortuna, to waken from your dream,
And share water of all life!

Light the candles, and say:

I speak for the fire!
This was the gift
Of the gods
That brought us out of the dark
And made us human beings;
With fire we began
To remake the world.
I call on you Fortuna
To find the fire within,
The magickal flame
Of self-transformation.
May I make my own fortune
With the power of my will!

Touch again the wheel, see it fill the universe, and say:

Of old our people ever spoke
Of fire, water, earth, and air.
That energy is what forms
The liquid, the solid, and the gaseous states.
All matter is star stuff
Of the primal creation;

All life on earth is one!
We are kin to
The birds of the air,
The fish of the sea,
The beasts of the forest.
All share our blood,
Our breath,
Our birth.
All live upon the wheel
O Fortuna!
May I hold the wheel!
May I live in the center!
May I embody thee, Bona Fortuna!

Stand and spin as the wheel spins with you. Become the wheel, become fate. Become karma; become Fortuna! Glow with golden power, and then stop and say:

I am Fortuna!
I rule the fates and am that which connects all things in the universe!
I am whirling galaxy!
I am spinning mandala of life!
I am the wheel of karma and balance
I am Fortuna Primigeneia, the firstborn
May I ever be new and lovely!
I am Fortuna Muliebris, goddess of women
May I ever be blessed with goddess power!
I am Fortuna Scribunda, the fate who writes
May my every word bring good fortune!
I am Fortuna Regia, goddess of rulership
May I ever rule Fate and embody true will!
I am Bona Fortuna, good fate
I give my blessings to all I love!
I am Agatha, the benevolent
For love given is always returned!
Fiat Fortuna!

Slowly turn. You are Fortuna, the glowing wheel of life. As a sun, see the beams of light fly from you bringing luck and good fortune wherever you wish them to go. Bless whomever you will with this good luck!

When done, slowly turn three times counterclockwise. Retract the power and slowly come "back to earth." Then sit, becoming a happier and luckier you than before. Say:

> *I offer the golden energy*
> *To the good fortune of all,*
> *In our mother's Fortuna's living body*
> *I find my own rebirth!*
> *Each human being is evolving,*
> *Fast or slow is our choice.*
> *Not to change is to pass away.*
> *And create it.*
> *This is the dance*
> *That life intended;*
> *I flow with her music*
> *And all will be well.*
> *Bona Rota! Bona Fortuna—fiat!*

Blow out the candle first. Then put the coins away, scatter the other items, and then go be lucky!

THE GODDESS

Freya

ORIGIN: Norse
ATTRIBUTES: fertility and new life
COLOR: light green
SYMBOL: golden necklace or swan
ELEMENT: air
STONE/METAL: smoky quartz or amber
SCENT: cedar

INTRODUCTION

She is fertility, the pure essence of life! You can feel the power of the goddess fill you every spring as all the animals and plants about you mate and give birth in a profusion of new life! If you are seeking to invoke fertility for yourself, for someone else, or for the living things around you, Freya is who you need! Her name means "lady," and she is the goddess of new life!

The lady Freya was the most widely worshipped form of the goddess in the Scandinavian countries (Norway, Sweden, and Denmark). She was also known throughout the British Isles and Germany, as well as the many other places colonized by the Vikings. A wild and romantic figure, she ruled over many aspects of life: all forms of lovemaking and the poetry associated with it, as well as the fertility of people, animals, and crops. She was leader of the valkyries or sword maidens, who flew over battlefields to give victory and choose the slain. She also gave to mankind a form of magick known as *seidhr*. This magick was very shamanic, and involved practices such as trance work, shape-changing, and traveling in the spirit body, as well as prophecy, healing, and the bringing of fertility.

Freya herself was the most beautiful of goddesses, and always wore the necklace brisingamein, made for her by four dwarves who may have been symbols of the four quarters of the world. She would sometimes fly in her feather cloak, which gave her the form of a falcon. At other times she traveled in her chariot, which was drawn by cats. Her twin brother was Frey, whose name means "lord." Among her other names were *gefn* ("giver"), *heidhr* ("bright one"), *mardoll* ("moon on the sea"), *lofn* ("love"), and *vanadis* (goddess of the Vanir).

Freya is a form of the very ancient earth mother who gave life and fertility to the land as bride of the sky father. Stories are told of her wanderings to find her lord when he was lost. It is said that when she wept for him her tears of gold fell upon the land, and that they turned to amber when they fell in the sea. Despite this, she is a lady of joy and very great power, sometimes associated with the sun herself.

As mother of new life, it is she who is called upon to help women conceive, help herds and flocks prosper, and increase the harvest of the crops.

★ ★ ★ ★ ★

Invocation of the Goddess Freya

Freya of the Vanir, whose name is the life of the world!
I call on the queen of light and of love,
Who shines like the sun on the earth and the sea!
Bring forth new life to me
Gift me with fertility!

You soar above in falcon form,
Cloaked in feathers of gold;
A secret hidden from the eyes of men,
A mystery known only to the heart.

Wanderer over the wide world's span
Weeping tears of gold and amber,
Tears of sorrow and joy!
When love long lost is found again
And the buried seeds are reborn and rising,
Bring forth new life to me
Gift me with fertility!

Bring new life to the trees clothed in leaves
And make the orchards ripe with fruit;
Grow tall the crops that feed the folk
In golden waves of wheat and corn
Quicken the wombs that will it
Bring new beings to the world
Bring forth new life to me
Gift me with fertility!

I call on you as the lady of love,
Fair goddess of springtime garbed in green
With arms as white as the birch tree's bark;
Whose form shines like moonlight
On the silver mirror of the still sea
When the winds are silent as night.
From your love let new life grow,
Let planted seeds rise tall and strong
Bring forth new life to me
Gift me with fertility!

I call on you to guard the living
And hold safe the boundaries of the wildwood;
Watch over the land where the tall trees stand
And the grasses cover the meadows
While bright flowers come again in spring
Bring forth new life to me
Gift me with fertility!

I call on you as magick maker,
Who journeys far-seeing in hidden ways

To know the future as well as the past!
In your cauldron you brew the love spell
As you chant the holy runes,
You bless with charms your chosen ones.
Witch-queen of sorceries dark and bright,
All-giver of the growing green,
Grant us the power of your enchantments!
Bring forth new life to me
Gift me with fertility!

By the holy well that sustains the worlds,
The well that lies at the roots of the tree of life,
May all trees grow strong as they drink
The sacred waters,
May all life be made strong by the magick of your love!
Bring forth new life to me
Gift me with fertility!

I call you as goddess of fertility
Who makes the crops rise tall!
Dancer in the growing fields
Whose hair is as gold as the ripening grain,
Freya the sister of sun-bright Frey;
You ride the boundaries of the land
In your chariot drawn by great cats!
The trees of the orchard blossom and fruit
With apples of gold that give youth eternal
To the gods and the children of men!
Bring forth new life to me
Gift me with fertility!

Lady of all the beasts and their birth,
Who watches over the nests and the caves
Cradles and soft beds
Where the young are concealed in safety;
You make the rivers run silver with salmon
And the trees birth leaves of new green,

You bring blessings of life to the land!
Bring forth new life to me
Gift me with fertility!

Most beautiful goddess desired by all,
Fairer than moon, sun, and stars,
Ringed about with the circle of blazing fire
Which is the necklace brisingamein!
Lady of wealth and plenty outpoured
From the wellspring that never runs dry,
Ever full of the life-giving waters;
Pour out your love and power upon us
Bring forth new life to me
Gift me with fertility!
Fehu! Freya! Dagaz!

* * * * *

$\mathcal{G}$oddess Freya Visualization Exercise

At the beginning of time
At the center of all the worlds
The great tree Yiggdrasill arises,
Broad of trunk, green of leaf,
Sheltering all living things.
Stronger than time are its branches;
Neither fire nor iron can harm it.
At its crown is an eagle,
Whose wings birth the winds.
At its roots coil serpents,
In the well of living waters.
From its wood were man and woman formed,
And from within it shall new life arise
Even after the end of all things
When the moon and the sun are fallen from the sky.
The tree holds all things in its embrace;
Past, present, and future are born

In the rivers that run from it
To the four quarters of the holy earth.
All other trees of the forest are its image,
For every place is the center of things.
All children of the human race are its kin,
Its sap is the blood of our veins.
Each human being is formed as a tree:
Our feet touch the earth like roots,
Our arms embrace the winds,
And the water of life runs through us all.
Feel now the force and the form of the tree,
Ever rising to reach the sun,
Embracing the life-giving golden light
With spreading branches and emerald leaves!
Cast out your mind across the globe
And feel the rhythm of that heart;
In the fruits of the orchards
And the cultivated crops of the fields;
In the newly conceived children
In all the life and growth of earth,
Riding the rhythms of the lady's loving heart
In an ever-growing tide of fertility.
Feel the driving energy of that life,
Rising through the roots of every plant,
Every animal
Feel the force of life and growth,
Ever expanding, ever spreading outward;
Feel the light of the green
Filling everything with fertilizing power;
Bringing new shoots out of barren wasteland,
Sprouting new life in womb and herd and field.
Feel the force of the soft blades of grass
Which crack open the concrete of the city's sidewalks.
The sperm and ovum dancing and joining
Feel the power of the growing life

Circling the entire living globe,
And breathe in its energy for a time.

★ ★ ★ ★ ★

$\mathcal{G}$ODDESS EMPOWERMENT RITUAL OF FREYA: CELEBRATION OF NEW LIFE AND FERTILITY

This empowerment ritual should be done outside, in a place of great life and abundance. If it has to be done inside, fill the room with flowers, plants, animals, and all living things. As you are seeking an empowerment of a great goddess of fertility, decide beforehand what this means to you and what you will to do with this energy. If you are a fertile woman, you may be "asking for" children! Or you may choose to take her power upon yourself so that you can grant fertilizing power to friends, family, livestock, crops, or whatever you wish! When you become Freya, you hold the gift of new life—enjoy!

You Will Need
◉ green clothing and a necklace of gold to wear
◉ an image of Freya
◉ flowers
◉ a shell or bowl
◉ cedar incense or cedar bark to burn
◉ matches
◉ a gold-colored cup of wine or mead (her traditional drink)
◉ a golden apple
◉ some seeds (any kind)
◉ a pot with earth in it (if you are inside)

The Ritual
Do this rite on a Friday (Freya's day!) at midday.

Meditate on life, new life, fertility, and the joy of this power.

When you are calm, imagine yourself as a tree. Visualize it deeply. This invokes the image of the great tree of life itself, which stands at the center of the world in so many mythological systems. In this ritual, the specific image is that of this tree (Yggdrasill) from Norse or Scandinavian mythology. This is followed by the invocation of Freya, queen of life and fertility in the earth and the sea, and of the light of the sun. Make an altar and place on it the image or symbol of Freya and surround it with flowers. Place the incense in the shell or bowl. Light it and circle yourself clockwise with it three times, saying:

> I cast this circle as a ring of fire,
> A force of protection to bring new life!
> As a turning wheel about this place
> Where seeds are planted to grow strong in time,
> As the womb of the goddess where life is born,
> I cast this circle as a ring of fire!

At each direction say:

> I call the winds from the East,
> That shake the leaves of the trees of night!
>
> I call the fires of the South,
> As sunlight calling the green to rise!
>
> I call the waters of the West,
> That run through the roots from the deepest well!
>
> I call on earth in the North,
> As power of stone and sustaining soil!

Sit in silence for a few moments, breathing deeply. Pour out some of the mead or wine, and say:

> Of old the lady of the northern lights
> Was called Freya in lands of fire and ice
> Mighty goddess of love and fertility
> Beautiful and terrible to see
> Ringed about with brilliant fire
> Her necklace is of amber and gold
> She rides the worlds and the winds and the waves
> In a chariot drawn by great cats.
> The silent places of life are hers
> And the secret homes and caves of beasts and humans.

She is giver of life
The light of the moon on the sea.
She offers to all the drink from her cup
And the names of all children are known to her.

Now chant for a time, rocking back and forth:
Shining Freya, magick's queen, we call you here!
Shining Freya, magick's queen, we call you here!
Shining Freya, magick's queen, we call you here!

Stand and go to the eastern edge of your circle. Slowly walk a spiral into the center, silently calling the power of Freya. When you reach the center, say:
The well at the roots of the tree is one
With every wellspring of the world.
The waters that flow
From the tree of life
Run through every living being.
As we drink together
Of the waters of life
We are one with all that lives.

Drink deeply of the cup and feel Freya's power enter you! Drink deep! Take a huge bite out of the apple and chew slowly. You are filled with the power of fertility, green and gold, shimmering! Stand and say:
I am Freya!
The great one, the gold one, the green one, the lady!
My cloak is of feathers and giant cats take me across the world!
I am the tree of life!
I fill all
With the seeds of new life,
And plant the children, foals, and new crops
On hills and in valleys,
In caves, barns, and homes
I give to all
The mother's flesh,
In the sun's embrace,

> *I grant fertility*
> *That the children may dance*
> *In the forests of forever!*

Now dance a spiral out, singing:

> *I am shining Freya, magick's queen, my touch is life!*
> *I am shining Freya, magick's queen, my touch is life!*
> *I am shining Freya, magick's queen, my touch is life!*

Now, take up the seeds and plant them in moist earth, either in the ground or in the pot you have provided. As Freya, you are bringing new life and fertility! Clearly visualize who or what you wish to receive this new life power. Meditate on this.

When you come back to being "you," place all the new energy into these now planted seeds and say:

> *Seeds in the womb of the mother earth,*
> *Grow strong in the sunlight of father sky!*
> *Root to trunk, branch to leaf, flower and fruit*
> *In the lady's name!*
> *Let all the worlds be bound together*
> *In life and love forever,*
> *Let the new life grow tall*
> *In the dance of seasons and the turning year.*
> *Blessed be, Laukaz!*
> *In Freya's name!*

Pour out the rest of the mead or wine, bury the incense, and touch the earth, thanking Freya!

THE GODDESS

Gaia

ORIGIN: Greek
ATTRIBUTES: protecting home and garden
COLOR: olive
SYMBOL: a standing stone or the planet Earth
ELEMENT: earth
STONE/METAL: agate
SCENT: myrrh

INTRODUCTION

She is the great mother, the personification of all nature and the supreme being of our planet. She was known as the great earth mother in Greek mythology, along with other names such as Gaia, (or Gaea), which means "broad bosomed," Great Mother, Universal Mother, Mother Earth, Primeval Prophetess, and Earth Deity. Her chief areas of power are motherhood, fertility, agriculture, marriage, prosperity, and healing. She is the goddess of the garden, home, and all earthy things! Gaia will give you a feeling of belonging and being one with the Earth. Gaia is the ultimate earth mom, an organic food–loving, save-the-planet type of deity.

In Greek history she is described as the "primal mother of the gods," the first mother before all other deities whose origins are lost in time.

Her familiar symbol was the sacred snake, which emerges from the earth with messages from the mother.

Gaia survived from a much earlier pantheon of gods as evidenced by the creation myths surrounding her. In the beginning were chaos and Gaia. Gaia alone gave birth to Uranus, the sky, and then together they bred the twelve titans. These ancient gods, mostly superseded by the Olympian gods, were said to be the originators of humankind and the inventors of the arts and magick.

And so the great mother Gaia seems as if she is reawakening in the human consciousness. We call on her to empower us as a power of the Earth, to help protect out home and to make our gardens and all green areas safe and prosperous. May her glory expand and may she increase our consciousness of the Earth!

* * * * *

INVOCATION OF THE GREAT MOTHER GAIA

Ma . . . ma . . . ma
Greatest mother of all
Source of all life
Source of all nourishment
Source of all reality
Open us now to your all-embracing wisdom.

As the wind blows about your body
As the trees which are your hairs sway
Feeling your perfumed breeze
We breathe as one.

As the earth below me sighs
The loam and grasses that are your flesh
The stones and boulders that are your bones
I touch the source of my very being
We live as one.

As the rivers and oceans murmur
Your blood and tears and elixir so sweet
The waters pulsing through your veins

I drink the essence of your vitality
We move and flow as one.

As the pulsing heart of you bursts with heat and magma
Your inner life a mirror of the sun's gentle fire
We burn and bloom as one.

We invoke you Io Evoe!
Great Goddess Gaia of the summer.
In the smell of riotous blossoms
Red and gold and blue and pink
We invoke you as the ripening life,
Newborn animals and ripe fruits abundant
We feel you in the ease and richness of a summer day.
The joy of buzzing bees and ripening grain
We invoke every memory, sense, and joy of summer
And so we invoke you, Great Mother Earth!

We invoke you Io Evoe!
Great Goddess Gaia of the autumn.
We see you in the colorful leaves that turn and fall,
Great swaths of brilliance painted upon the trees.
The smell of rich earth ready for the cold
You are seen in the storing of food by the animals,
By the protecting of shelters, homes, and burrows,
You are savored in the harvested fruits and baking bread
In the rich wine and fall feasts of delight
With you we prepare and revel
Awaiting the time of silence and wonder.
Thankful for your abundance and life.
We invoke every memory, sense, and joy of autumn
And so we invoke you, Great Mother Earth!

We invoke you Io Evoe!
Great Goddess Gaia of the winter.
We feel you as the blanket of cold covers the green,
As the sleeping of the animals and the fleeing of birds,
In the lonely echo of ice and pine

As the sigh of life rebuilding, renewing, refocusing,
The chill of sharp midnight's cold and full of stars
The joy of walking through evergreen-scented hills and valleys
We taste you in the ice-cold spring water flavored with snow
And in the flavorful foods of winter.
We remember you, o Gaia, with yule log, holly, and tree alight
We invoke every memory, sense, and joy of winter
And so we invoke you, Great Mother Earth!

We invoke you Io Evoe!
Great Goddess Gaia of the spring.
We invoke you as the earth reborn, as light green amidst brown
The smell of thawing brooks and first blooms,
The cry of newborn animals in the meadows,
The feel of spring showers and parting clouds,
As life returning to the buds of every branch
The unfurling ferns and the curling vines
You are tasted in the first leaves and vegetables
The fresh herbs and teas of healing and contentment
Shaking out of your slumber we hear you
In the call of the returning fowl and songbirds,
In the howl of mating and the rutting of the new deer.
We invoke every memory, sense, and joy of spring
And so we invoke you, Great Mother Earth!

Mother of all seasons
Of hearth, home, and garden
It is ever to the earth that we return.
Our life is spent living with you,
Working upon you,
Taking nourishment from you,
Returning to you,
Without you we could not live.

Great Mother Gaia
Open your arms
That we may embrace you and become renewed.
Open your heart

That we may feel joy that comes of nature.
Open your mind
That we may be protected in your embrace,
That our gardens, fields, and woods may prosper
In right feeling
Right thought
And right deed
Io Gaia, Io Evoe!

★ ★ ★ ★ ★

$\mathcal{G}$ODDESS GAIA VISUALIZATION EXERCISE

There is light
Infinite and unyielding
Forever and timeless
Pure light and pure consciousness.
Then you feel a tugging,
A vague drifting,
A slow beginning of time
A glimmering of consciousness of space.
And the pull becomes stronger
Until with a great wrenching thrust
You are sent spinning into darkness.
The light quickly fades
Until all you see is a large disc of light
And the glowing flickering flames that surround you
And the infinite darkness surrounding you.
Slowly the trauma of separation begins to fade,
You and the ball of light begin to spin
You begin to dance about each other
You begin to notice other bits of light
Floating around you in the darkness.
Age after age passes as you slowly dance around each other
The orbits become more regular
The movements settle into a pattern
You yourself shed protruding bits of matter.

This becomes a droplet that dances around you,
You are sculpting your body with motion
Rounding your body with shaking and shifting.
In your heart is the once infinite light,
Part of the globe of light before you
Pulsing with the beat of the dance.
As your skin cools and hardens,
As your flesh buckles rises and bunches
You begin to breathe with a new life.
Smoke and gases flying about your skin,
Trapped in the dance
Soon clouds form as your breathing increases.
From the clouds comes rainstorms and lightning
Storm after storm, age after age
Until there is a moment that stands still.
Within the storm is a flash of light,
A star between heaven and earth,
A seed of the first infinite white light consciousness,
And there is something new that you have given birth to,
Something that grows upon you
Something that is of you and yet is other.
It replicates and changes,
The one becomes many and the variations increase.
First they are clear and then come the many colors.
Blue and green begin to clothe your body
And soon your skin is covered with this thing called life.
It pulses and hums with your dance.
Delighted, you weave new songs which find reflection in life.
Forms flourish or fade,
Note by note the seasons change
When you sleep all sleeps with you,
When you awake all blooms and begins to move.
For ages the dance and song grows in complexity
But you are ever and always the mother,
The songweaver and the holder of all life.
All things grow and take nourishment from you,

All things perish and return to feed you.
You are forever the life of life
The protector of every home,
Every garden,
Every person who calls you.
You are Gaia!

* * * * *

THE GRAND EMPOWERMENT RITUAL OF GAIA: HONORING AND BEING PROTECTED BY THE MOTHER EARTH

Gaia is the Earth personified. To become this deep primal "Earth Mother" is to *become* the power of the planet.

In keeping with the power of this hip mama goddess, a feast is called for!

You Will Need

◉ a round fresh loaf of bread (handmade if possible, with fresh ingredients such as herbs and berries)

◉ a small drum

◉ matches

◉ green cloth (center), candle (to South), shell of water (West), stone (North), cedar bark (East), all of these to be placed on the green cloth

Place the bread in center of the four directions. Stand and be still. Visualize the power of Mother Earth encircling you. Then, touch the bread, saying:

This is the body of the Earth
This is the flesh of the world
This is the foundation of nourishment
This is the spirit of mother nature

Gaia!
All one mother

> *Be here now*
> *Io Evoe!*

Begin to beat the drum at will. After a time, when you truly feel the earth Spirit is present, light the cedar. bark. Hold up the smoking bark and say:

> *This is the breath of the mother*
> *The scent of her eternal becoming*
> *Honor to the winds of mother earth*
> *May they bless and empower me!*
> *Gaia!*
> *All one mother*
> *I am thee!*
> *Io Evoe!*

Bless yourself with the smoke by waving it about your body. Feel the winds of the Earth upon you. Say:

> *I breathe the breath of Gaia*
> *Gaia and I are one!*

Replace it and take up the candle.

Feel the inner magma core of the Earth. Light the candle and say:

> *This is the fire of the mother*
> *Her magma heart and web of energy*
> *Honor to the fires of mother earth!*
> *May they bless and empower me!*
> *Gaia!*
> *All one mother*
> *I am thee!*
> *Io Evoe!*
>
> *I feel the heat of Gaia*
> *Gaia and I are one*

Blow out the candle. Take up the shell with water. Feel the oceans of the Earth in your blood. Say:

> *This is the blood of the mother*
> *The primal substance of life and death*
> *Honor to the waters of mother earth*

May they bless and empower me!
Gaia!
All one mother
I am thee!
Io Evoe!

Taste the water, saying:
I drink the blood of Gaia
Gaia and I are one!

Replace the shell. Pick up the stone. Feel the forests, mountains, and soil of the Earth as your flesh. Say:
These are the bones of the mother
The earth-touch of her permanence
Honor to the flesh of mother earth
May it bless and empower me!
Gaia!
All one mother
I am thee!
Io Evoe!

Touch the stone to your heart, saying:
I feel the bones of Gaia
Gaia and I are one!

Play your drum, a sacred offering to Gaia. With the rhythm feel yourself becoming the earth. You are the rhythm of the winds, the oceans, the inner magma fires, the shifting earth. You are Gaia!

Then, stand and say:
The breezes of Gaia are my breath (breathe)
The striving of Gaia is my energy (stretch toward the sun)
The drinking root of Gaia is my inspiration (dig feet into earth)
The loam and stones of Gaia are my flesh (kneel and touch the earth)

I am Gaia
One earth, one body, one mind, one spirit
One consciousness
Blessing my land

My home
My loved ones!
Blessing upon all the Earth!

Lay facedown on the earth, hands outstretched. Meditate upon how you are Gaia and the Earth. When done, take up the bread and eat it; it is your body. You honor all beings.

You may give pieces of this bread later to loved ones. Scatter it in a garden to bless it or leave some in your home to bless it. The last piece is to be buried in the earth.

When you're ready to close your empowerment ritual, stand and say:
Honor to the mother
Who gives us life and love
Honor to the mother
Who teaches us and nourishes us
Honor to the mother
Source of life and death and survival
Mother Earth we thank you
Gaia mother Earth
Be with us now and forever!
Heal the earth rebirth!
Io Evoe!

Touch the earth three times and then depart as a true child of the Great Mother Earth.

THE GODDESS
Hecate

ORIGIN: Greek
ATTRIBUTE: protecting women and dogs, and cursing the unjust
COLOR: midnight blue or burgundy
SYMBOL: a torch (sometimes two) or a dog
ELEMENT: earth
STONE/METAL: onyx
SCENT: dittany of Crete or mastic

INTRODUCTION

Hexes or curses, anyone? Tired of playing nice and want to strike back once and for all? Want to explore the dark side of the goddess in a positive way *and* get some justice? Hecate is the dark mother of fate or karma, you could say. Calling upon her helps you come to terms with your shadow or dark side. We all have dark parts of ourselves, and these are very important parts of our being. Without shadow, there is no light. Learn and grow from your darker feelings and emotions. Hecate will help reveal your true self to you and the dark fountain of power you can use.

Hecate is a pre-Greek goddess, one of the oldest that survived into classical Greek culture, and even today she is still popular. One of her myths is very key to understanding her. All-seeing Hecate witnessed

Hades abducting the goddess of new life, Persephone, into the under-world. Demeter, Persephone's mother, was beside herself searching for her lost daughter. Hecate found Demeter and told her what she had witnessed. Leading Demeter by the hand, Hecate's torches lit the way as they descended into hell to rescue Persephone from Hades. Hecate was thus known as a friend of women and children, and a protector of those who called on her. Hecate will go after anyone who has harmed any innocent, be it woman, child, or dog. To curse in her name is to demand fairness and retribution.

Hecate is known by many names, such as Goddess of the Dark Moon, Queen of the Night, and later as the Witch's Queen, as she was renamed in the Middle Ages. Hecate is a true triple goddess: maiden, mother, crone all in one. Her three masks are the faces of a horse, a dog, and a lion or a serpent. In her hand she holds one or two torches that light the way. The name Queen of the Witches is also associated with Halloween. In fact, this holiday is sacred to Hecate, as are bats, spiders, toads, willow trees, and tombstones.

Getting the picture? Hecate is a little spooky. As guardian of the crossroads, it is said that she is worshipped as the triple goddess so she can stand and watch different ways at the same time. Worshippers often left offerings of hay and bread to Hecate at the crossroads.

Hecate was also the guardian of deceased souls. In her crone aspect, Hecate is the goddess who haunts graveyards, crime scenes, and tombs with her infernal hounds. All dogs are sacred to her. Enchantments, spells, and hexes are ruled by her.

Woman used to invoke Hecate for protection from evil when leaving their homes. This, of course, was in the days before mace and self-defense classes. Still, it is not a bad idea if you get an uncomfortable feeling when you are in a parking lot alone at night to call out her name. Nobody would dare to mess with you when you howl her name.

Hecate guards the gateway to the underworld and is able to aid you in contacting departed loved ones and animals, especially dogs. Hecate in her mother aspect is the goddess of childbirth. She protects women in labor. Hecate also watches over midwives and all who care for women and children. Hecate in her maiden form is a dark moon goddess. Hecate was given the gift to keep or give whatever she wanted to humanity.

Hecate is the only Greek goddess on equal footing with Zeus, king of the gods, probably because of her age and because she was always invoked when the gods met. Hecate is used for protection and to curse those who harm others, especially women, children, and dogs. If you have been misled or harmed by anyone, especially by men, Hecate is the one to help you to set the record straight with hexes and curses.

* * * * *

$\mathcal{G}$ODDESS HECATE INVOCATION

Io Evoe Hekate!
O Hecate I invoke thee
Stand at the crossroads
And I howl like a wolf
At a full moon
Calling your name.

Beautiful Hecate
In maiden form
With long black hair and white skin
Wearing a long flowing robe of burgundy
I invoke thee for strength in all endeavors.

Maternal Hecate
In the mother form
Lovely loving
Protectress of pregnant
Women and guardian
Of the threshold of life
I invoke thee
For healthy babies, and healthy mothers
Who prosper and cry coming into this world
Embracing life and being born.

Crone Hecate
Who is a wizened ancient
Crooked like a willow tree
Bending in the wind

Seer of all and Queen of Witches
Knowing all secrets of life and death
I invoke thee to see deep into the past
And beyond the future.
It is through you that I may speak
To my ancestors
And to unborn generations.

I invoke you, O guardian goddess
Of the animal kingdom.
Your three masks
Lioness of protection
Dog of childbirth
Horse of freedom
Other animals gather
At your side while I call
Your name O Hecate!
Toads hop
Spiders weave their webs
The hounds howl
All is as it should be.
Friend to mother and children
You reunited Demeter with
Persephone when Hades dared
To take her to the Underworld.
With your torch you lit the way
And led Demeter to her daughter Persephone.
Full moon, dark moon, crescent moon
All show the shadows that you walk in unafraid
Of any living or dead creature.
To some you appear young
With long black hair, white skin,
And a long burgundy robe.
To others you are the mother of childbirth
And happy healthy babies and mothers.
I invoke your name
When I go out into the evening

Knowing that I am not afraid
A strong protector are you
Men fear your powers
You walk confident wherever you go
Io Evoe!
Hecate, ever watchful
Of all worlds
Traveling to the heavens, earth,
And down below.
You stands at the crossroads
Queen of mysteries
Queen of the witches
Goddess of all
Hold thy torch high Hekate!
Banish all fear!
Protect me and mine!
Blast and destroy all enemies!
Kyria Hekate!

* * * * *

$\mathcal{G}$oddess Hecate Visualization Exercise

It is night,
The moon is full above you.
You travel a foggy road.
At the crossroads you stop
You see her standing in the dark, hooded
Torches raised in both hands
Dogs quietly at her feet.
All-knowing, all-seeing goddess
Queen that can see three ways
Maiden, mother, crone
Of the three worlds
Earth, heaven, hell
Yet you are one mother, maiden, crone.
One face is a lion, another is a dog, the other is a horse

All three are your protectors.
Now the hounds of Hecate are beside you,
Howling their haunting melody.
Whisper the dark deed you need
Tell her the curse you must send
The evil that must be destroyed.
Now hear the eerie silence after
The dogs' cries stop.
This is the goddess Hecate
Sometimes in graveyards she
Hides behind tombstones
Waiting for the departed to pause and ask
Directions to the other side.
She lead souls to their next path
Torch in hand.
Woman of mysteries and metaphysics
Who sees all and knows all.
Equal to Zeus
She is a shadow, a veil, a darkness
That holds you and helps you.
Hecate can do all.
Dreams, hopes, and desires.
Hecate can give any gift,
Hecate can take away any gift.
Be careful what you ask for.
Listen to her whispers; leave her a simple flower
Then retreat from the crossroads
Into the mist
Through the woods
Back
To yourself
In silence.

Goddess Hecate Empowerment Ritual: Becoming and Using the Shadow

This is where you get to become the great Goddess Hecate. No, you will not all of a sudden end up with three heads. What you will receive is a powerful jolt of your dark side, the source of inner dark strength that is used for cursing and defense. It is wise to choose which aspect of Hecate you would like to be. If you want to become the maiden, you should wear something sexy and witchy. If you chose the mother, it is important to wear a robe or something burgundy. Maybe as the crone dress up like a hag, warts and all. It is possible to combine all three looks by wearing whatever you want as long as it is black. Anything spooky goes.

You Will Need

◉ matches
◉ a small torch or large candle
◉ some musk oil
◉ some dark wine mixed with a little of your blood
and a small black cup to put it in
◉ some dark purple flowers and fruit
◉ an image of Hecate

The Ritual

Do this ritual at a crossroads or in a garden where you can draw a crossroads on the ground. The moon should be full or near full. If you must do this inside, do it in a basement and draw a crossroads on the floor with flour. This is the crossroads where you will be standing and become Hecate. If you have a dog bring it along. Stand at the crossroads and light the torch or candle. Raise your hands high and say:

> I call you, O Hecate, creature of the night
> O fearless goddess of the unborn
> I stand at the crossroads
> With your hounds at my side
> O Hecate
> I summon your animal shades!

Fill this center with power!
Power of the three heads
The nocturnal ones, reptiles, snakes, and toads.
Powerful dogs and horses
Dragons, lions, and serpents!
Rise up the realm of darkness
O Hecate come!
Io Evoe Hecate!
Nox Dea!

Pour out some of the oil and anoint yourself on your pulse points with it. Pour out some wine and blood into the black cup and drink your fill. Feel the goddess swirl about you as a cloud of dark power, comforting and protecting you, filling you with power. Spin around and feel the forces becoming you. You are Hecate, the Dark Lady! The shadow fills you; and you become the shadow! Be still, take up the torch in your left hand, and say:

I am Hecate!
I see all watching
A three-headed goddess am I
Maiden wears a horse mask
An independent Night-Mare am I.
As mother I wear a dog mask
Dogs give birth easily
And slay all who threaten.
As a crone I wear a lioness mask
A fierce huntress and guardian am I.
I am three
Three in one
The power of three am I
Heiros Heiros Heiros!
Hecate am I!

I, Hecate, who watches and waits
Head held high above all
Deep below the surface
Underneath the ground
Lie hidden meanings

Not wanting to be revealed
All is profound.
Need an answer to a question?
Want a problem resolved?
Then ask me, Hecate
Queen of the witches
And ruler of all!

Look into the black cup of wine and blood. See what visions lie there for you, then face to the right and say:

I see all watching
None dare harm a mother or child
Under my protection

The power of childbirth
Dogs are my familiars
I protect midwives
I say birth is fast and painless
I, Hecate, give the greatest gift
The gift of life
Io Hecate!

Now face left to the torch and say:

I, Hecate, give life
And I also take it away
If a loved one has passed
I, Hecate, will take their soul away
I speak to the dead
I have hidden knowledge
I know the unknown
In shadows
Io Hecate!

Look deeply into the torch. Speak to the dead, if you will. You will hear their voices in the hiss of the flame. Then look up into the darkness and say:

I am Hecate and hear my curse!
Woe to the man

Who causes trouble
Even Hades is cautious of me
He steps out of my way when he sees me come.

If the desire is do or die
When all else has failed
I, mighty Hecate,
Will answer all problems
And no one is denied.

Be watchful what you ask
I give and also take
I am Queen of the Witches
I am fair and mighty!
Oai! Oai! Oai!
I curse those who hurt those I love!

Look deeply again into the cup. Focus on all who have harmed and need karmic punishment. Spit into the cup and pour it out on the ground. Hecate has spoken!

Sit quietly and learn what Hecate has to teach you. When you are done, come back to being "you." Then offer fruit, flowers, and oil to the image of Hecate in thanks, saying:

O Hecate!
Queen of the crossroads!
Lady of owl, snake, and bat
Hound of the shadow!
Guard me!
Protect me from evil!
Give boons and blessings!
Destroy those who hurt
Enemies of women and children!
Thank you for your lovely shadow, O Hecate!
Kyria Hecate!

Now blow out the torch, howl at the moon, and then depart.

THE GODDESS
Hestia

* * * * * * * * * * * * * * * * * *

ORIGIN: Greek
ATTRIBUTE: happy hearth, home, and family
COLOR: orange/yellow
SYMBOL: fireplace/hearth (with flame)
ELEMENT: fire
STONE/METAL: carnelian
SCENT: sage

* * * * * * * * * * * * * * * * * *

INTRODUCTION

Are you a homebody? If you feel a strong sense of place and are, as one comedian put it, a domestic goddess, then you are already a devotee of Hestia! Call on her to receive, preserve, and make better in every way a home. She is the primal power of the sheltering Earth; become her and truly know that home is where the heart is.

Hestia is one of the oldest goddesses among the Greek gods, and is recognized as being among the most ancient of all beings. Her name means "hearth," the central fire of the home, and may be the oldest unifying symbol for the human race. It is said that Hestia was the first to teach mankind the building of houses, as well as many other domestic arts. The hearthstove in the kitchen and the nourishing food it provides is inevitably linked with the love and support given by parents. From the time we leave the womb and become separate flesh, our mothers are our first and primal love, the model for all our later relationships and the very basis of society.

From the earliest human settlements the hearth has been the core and place of assembly. Before the secret of actually making a fire was known, the preservation of the existing fires (sprung miraculously from the celestial lightning) was imperative to survival. The guardianship of fire was perhaps one of the major preserves of the ancient matriarchs and also a source of their authority in the tribe.

In the halls of ancient Olympus, the home of the gods, Hestia tended the sacred fire and opened all of their councils. She preserved the peace on numerous occasions, and the first victim of every sacrificial rite was always awarded to her. All through the ancient world the hearth of every home was thought of as an altar, the center of life, and the place where the ancestral spirits who watched over the family were worshipped. The temple fire was central to all ritual as well, and any suppliant who claimed sanctuary at the hearth of the city hall, the home, or the temple was placed under protection. Hospitality to guests, strangers or otherwise, was once a sacred obligation. All civic ceremonies and debates opened with her rites, and the Olympian gods themselves swore their oaths in her name. In times of mourning, the hearth fire was allowed to go out and ceremonially relit. In many parts of the world, all the household fires would be allowed to die out on certain festival occasions, and then rekindled by the whole community and distributed to each home.

The Greek philosopher and mathematician Pythagoras said that the fire of Hestia was the center of the Earth. She governed all altars and hearths, and all rituals began and ended with her invocation. We should perhaps recall that all life on our planet survives because of the molten core of magma that warms and sustains us.

Hestia was said to be the daughter of the primal deities Cronus and Rhea. Her Latin name was Vesta, and Rome's famous temple of the vestal virgins preserved an eternal flame thought to be essential to the survival of the city. These priestesses were highly honored at all major public events, and many elements of their practice were later adapted by Christian convents, although their own temple was destroyed.

The very word *hearth* is cognate to the Germanic *erde* or *herde,* meaning "earth"; and Hertha or Holda is a northern form of this same goddess of the Earth, to whom many ceremonies and customs of the home were devoted.

This goddess acts as protector of the people. We call upon her to guard our families from dangers in the home and without. More than protection, Hestia is the spirit of the home, the love, warmth, community, and nurturing of a harmonious and peaceful home.

* * * * *

*I*NVOCATION OF THE GODDESS HESTIA

Hestia! Hestia! Hestia!
We call you!

First mother of the world,
Primal one of birth!
Holder of the hearth fire,
Shelter of the Earth!

The central place where all gather;
A molten core sustains the globe
As the hearth fire warms all hearts.
All circles are formed
Around the flames, to dance.

Yours is the fire of every home,
Where elders wait
And children return
For the gathering celebration;
Where parenthood finds
The year's reward.

Yours is the flame on all altars
In church, synagogue, or mosque,
Temple, shrine, or household,
Where devotion's candles flame!

By the lighted lamp
Is worship found.

Yours is the light of wisdom
In school or college,
Of compassion in the houses of rulers
And inspiration of artists;
Yours the hands of skill
Which are ever making new things.

At the hearth all gather
In one family, in one love!

Most ancient one,
Who gives birth to all generations
And bears all forms of life!
You are the home of all,
The place of belonging
For every being
The shelter of nurturing and
Sacred togetherness
You are the peace of clan and family
Be here now!

Mother of the stones,
Womb of jewel and crystal,
Parent of the fertile soil
And of the high mountains,
Of the valleys of farmland
And the rolling hills of pasture,
Of the forests of uncounted trees
You are the home of all
The place of belonging
For every being
The shelter of nurturing and
Sacred togetherness
You are the peace of clan and family
Be here now!

Mother of the ocean realms,
Spawning ground of beginnings
And cauldron of evolution!
Where fields of plankton
Weave through the waving weeds,
Where shells move like living minerals
And eels writhe serpentine;
Where schools of fish in unending profusion
Dance their mating dance,
Great whales and dolphins ride the sunlit surface,
Not far below in the depths of time.
You are the home of all
The place of belonging
For every being
The shelter of nurturing and
Sacred togetherness
You are the peace of clan and family
Be here now!

Mother of beasts in every form
On all the wide-flung continents;
The predators and the prey
In their ceaseless dance of chase,
Their romance of concealment
And migration and mating!
The bear and wolf and hunting cat,
The ram and goat, the stag and bull,
The small wild things in their burrows
And the great apes of the trees;
The serpent, lizard, and turtle,
The motion of insect life!
You are the home of all
The place of belonging
For every being
The shelter of nurturing and
Sacred togetherness

You are the peace of clan and family
Be here now!

Mother of birds, who soars on the wind,
Who rides the currents of outer air
To wander in the clouds.
Eagle and songbird, owl and hawk,
With colored feathers glide;
Peacock in glory, vulture and swan,
Go their ways in harmony.
And joining the dance came human life.
You are the home of all
The place of belonging
For every being
The shelter of nurturing and
Sacred togetherness
You are the peace of clan and family
Be here now!

All these your bounty and your spawn,
At the hearth all gather
In one family, in one love!

First mother of the world,
Primal one of birth!
Holder of the hearth fire,
Body of the earth!

Most ancient one,
Who gives birth to all generations
And bears all forms of life!
You are the home of all
The place of belonging
For every being
The shelter of nurturing and
Sacred togetherness
You are the peace of clan and family
Be here now!

Io Phos! Hestia!

Hestia! Hestia! Hestia!
We call you!

★ ★ ★ ★ ★

GODDESS HESTIA VISUALIZATION EXERCISE

In the warm green glow
At the heart of the world
You float in fetal bliss,
Curled in a ball
Drifting in the waters
Warm as blood;
Before birth,
You dream in the womb.
The body of your mother
Is your entire universe,
Her flesh surrounding you
Is the infinite extent
Of all you know.
Her heartbeat unceasing
A rhythm shared,
Her movements
Your intimate dance.
The light that reaches you now
Seems red,
The fire of the outside world
Grows nearer to you.

Bird hatched from an egg,
You are born into light;
Growing stronger,
You soar above the earth.
As if from space you see the globe,
A wheel of turning hours and seasons,
A slow spinning out of fates.

The sea tides rise and fall,
The clouds weave their images,
All heated by the central fire
And heat of the life of earth.
You sense it,
Not so far beneath the surface;
The core of magma seething ceaselessly
Like a beating heart,
The channels of the lava's flow
Like bright veins of liquid gold
Running through the ridges of mountains
To spill in volcanic fire;
Lying quiet beneath the oceans
And warming the currents of the gulfs.

And from above this globe you see
The lights of home and workplace,
The centers of gathering and solitude
Where humanity dwells:
Always on the earth
And always in the light.
There are families and tribes,
Nations and races,
Communities of every size
Drawn together against the night,
Raising fires against the cold,
Creating life out of death.
We seek our beginnings
And cry out against endings,
All in the mother's embrace;
We cry out our differences
Though all are the same,
All in the mother's embrace;
One world,
One people,
One planet,
One life,

All in the mother's embrace.
And all our joining and conflict,
All our loving and struggle,
All our getting and spending
End all in the mother's embrace.

From the womb whence we came,
There we all shall return!

The light of peaceful home
Washes over all living beings
All find home
All find peace
So may it be.

★ ★ ★ ★ ★

GRAND EMPOWERMENT RITUAL OF HESTIA: BECOMING THE CLAN SPIRIT— THE DOMESTIC MOTHER GODDESS

This is a ritual to wrap around you the spirit or soul of your home, family, clan, and tribe, however you define it. This can mean your friends and relatives, fellow workers or worshippers, or your neighbors or countrymen. In the end, it means all human beings and the place called Earth that is our home. Hestia brings people together in peace and sharing, nurturing and shelter. If you wish to do these things in your life, become Hestia, the domestic goddess!

You Will Need
- matches
- dried bay leaves
- a small plate
- salt
- a white candle
- white flowers
- homemade bread or other baked item
- a ceramic cup of tap water

@ a drawn symbol of your family or tribe

@ an image of the home goddess (optional)

The Ritual

Before you begin, light a few dried bay leaves and let them smolder in a small plate. You will need to do this rite in your home, at your fireplace or in your kitchen. At the place you will call her, make a small circle of salt and place a white candle in the center with an image of Hestia surrounded by white flowers. Clap your hands three times and say:

> *I stand here to speak of Hestia,*
> *Who is called Vesta,*
> *Who is called Hertha,*
> *The mother of the world.*
> *Kyria Hestia!*
> *Bless me, bless my home, bless my family, bless my tribe!*
> *May we be as one with all kin*
> *In your light!*

Light the candle, saying:

> *I light the fire at the center,*
> *Because that is the first place of gathering*
> *And the coming together of the people.*
> *Here we are all one family.*
>
> *Hestia sanctifies the fire*
> *At the heart of every home.*
> *She lights the flame*
> *In the sanctuary of every religion.*
>
> *She is the center of all things*
> *And the boundary surrounding them as well.*
> *She is the heart of the world*
> *And the living body of flesh.*
>
> *She is the mother of the world*
> *And all who live upon her.*
> *She is the first being and will be the last.*
> *There is nothing which is not born from her.*

Visualize that you can scoop the heat of the flame in your hands and bathe yourself in its energy. Do this three times, and feel her light fill you. As you become the great goddess, your entire body becomes a flame of the sacred fire! Spread warmth and love to all, saying:

> *I am Hestia!*
> *I am Vesta!*
> *I am Hertha!*
> *Heiros gamos!*
> *Mine is the fire*
> *Which Prometheus won for us,*
> *The tool of change*
> *That made us human.*
>
> *It guarded us from the wild beasts*
> *And the terrors of the night;*
> *It is the cookfire giving plenty,*
> *And the offering place of the first sacrifice.*
>
> *It is the council fire where wisdom is shared,*
> *And the homefire where family gathers.*
> *It is the fire of the forge of making*
> *And the light of knowledge passed down through the ages.*
>
> *In ancient times the sacred flame*
> *Was the center of every temple, every town, every home;*
> *Ever burning and shared by all,*
> *The sign of true community.*
>
> *I gathered all family*
> *All clan*
> *All tribes*
> *All human beings*
> *About my sacred flame*
> *Of safety, shelter, and nurturing!*
> *Here I burn to unite our hands*
> *In the work of healing the earth,*
> *And to unite our hearts*
> *In peace and prosperity!*

As one family, one tribe.
I bless the home,
bless the family,
Bbless the tribe!
With light, life, love, and laughter!
May we be as one kin
In the light
Phos!
Hestia!
I am the light!

Hold the symbol you have drawn of your family or tribe in front of the candle, saying:

Here is the sign of our unity,
The symbol of our tribe.
Here is gathered a power
We all may share at need.
I bless and empower this
As the token of a whole
Which is greater than the sum of the parts.
The circle shall grow, and never be broken.
As I am the goddess of the hearth
May the winds of the East
And all the birds of the air witness it!
May the fires of the South
And the sun and moon and stars witness it!
May the waters of the West
And all the fishes of the sea witness it!
May the stones of the North
And all the beasts of the earth witness it!
May all the goddesses and gods
And the peoples of the world witness it!

Burn the symbol and let it finish burning on the plate of bay leaves. See all of those you love: your family, tribe, and all humans gathering about this flame, for this flame is the sacred light of unity. Toast this gathered and loving unity you have become with the water, saying:

May all drink deep! May they never thirst!

Now meditate upon the flame, the hearth, and the unity of family, tribe, and humanity.

When you are no longer Hestia but have again become "you," then toss a bit of salt and a flower to the four directions, sending the light of home and unity and peace to all, saying:

One family, one clan,
We have gathered here;
The circle opened
Can never be broken.

The fire kindled
Must now be shared,
The light shall shine
Warming every home!
Kyria Hestia!
Bless me, bless my home, bless my family, bless my tribe!
May we be as one kin
In your light of home!

Blow out the candle, but light it whenever you need unity or peace in your home, town, city, country, or in the world . . . feed the bread to all you love. May your home be filled with peace!

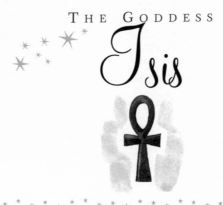

THE GODDESS

Isis

ORIGIN: Egyptian
ATTRIBUTE: developing psychic powers and divination
COLOR: dark blue
SYMBOL: ankh or thet (Egyptian symbols) or a throne
ELEMENT: water
STONE/METAL: lapis
SCENT: kyphi or jasmine

INTRODUCTION

Isis was and still is one of the most popular and most worshipped goddesses in the world. She is known as the mistress of magic and the lady of psychic powers and divination. Call upon her powers if you want to develop your inner psychic abilities, cast spells, or do any sort of divination or fortune-telling.

Her origins date back in Egyptian history to the earliest dynasties of the old kingdom when she was revered and worshipped. Isis has been called the queen of heaven, the mother of all the gods, the savior of all mankind, the mother of mysteries, the queen of the dead, the mistress of magick, sorceress, the bearer of wings, the red lady, queen of the crowns of South and North (kingdoms). In ancient Egypt, she was often called "one superior to whom the gods cannot be," mighty one of enchantments, form of the words of power, mother of the horizon of heaven, revealer of the mysteries of the stars, and many other titles!

She was always important but rose to become the most popular goddess of the ancient world during the late kingdom, the rise of imperial Greece and, later, throughout the expansion of the Roman Empire. During the late kingdom, the god Osiris and his cult became the most popular religious movement in Egypt, and Isis, as his wife and as the mother of Horus, his son (the pharaoh), became widely venerated. Later the mystery cults of Isis spread throughout the Greek and Roman Empires. Such greats as Plato, Aristotle, and Herodotus were initiated and wrote extensively about the power of her magickal abilities.

Over the centuries Isis absorbed the powers and identities of a number of lesser goddesses and became so multifaceted that she literally was every goddess. Maiden, mother, crone—she hid every form of woman behind her veil. Her aspect as the goddess of mysteries has been preserved and handed down to us today as the high priestess card of the tarot. A look at this trump will show you Isis the queen of magick and goddess of heaven. She is often depicted in Egyptian art as a beautiful goddess wearing the crowns of the northern and southern Egyptian kingdoms. She is often seen wearing the horned crown of Hathor with the solar disc between the horns. Sometimes she is shown wearing the single feather of the goddess Maat and sometimes she wears the uraeus, the serpent crown.

The most common symbol seen on the head of Isis is the throne. This is actually the glyph for her name and in many ways reveals the essence of her power. She literally was the throne upon which sat the pharaoh and spiritually represents the basis of all spiritual power. She often holds a papyrus scepter and/or a thet—this is a looped buckle or belt that signifies cycles, rebirth, and the womb.

In all myths, Isis is always the pivot around which all the gods circle. The myth of her husband, Osiris, is very popular. His brother Set coveted his throne and tricked him into trying out a coffin, and then tossed him into the Nile River. Isis found the body of her husband, but the god Set took it back and cut it into many pieces and scattered it. Isis, in mourning, set out and covered the earth seeking the pieces of Osiris. She assembled the pieces together, all but the phallus, which had been devoured by a crocodile. Then using the magick formula of life (given to her by Thoth or Ra) she fashioned a new phallus for her husband and brought him back to life. She then mated with him and become pregnant with Horus. Osiris faded to the underground, where he reigns forever as the lord of the dead. Isis then wandered across Egypt and was refused entrance to a house when she was in labor. She had to give birth with the animals in a manger (sound familiar?). Isis then hid in a swamp after giving birth because Osiris's brother sought to kill her child. She suckled and raised her child until he was old enough to fight Set. He did so and won. Thus her husband, son, and herself all became redeemers of the universe. She reigns in amenta (the underworld) with Osiris. She is the great mother goddess of all nature on earth and the reigning goddess of heaven as well.

May Mother Isis initiate, bless, and empower your psychic powers, your magicks, and your spiritual undertakings as you seek to grow and to part the veil of mysteries!

* * * * *

$\mathcal{G}$ODDESS ISIS INVOCATION

Tua ast!
Great goddess Isis
Wings multicolored
Filling the sky
The star has risen in the West
The Sun God Ra has bathed it in his blood.
The light falls upon a throne
And the waters of the earth burst forth
Sweet and healing and magickal
Fill me with the inner psychic power
May I see the hidden mysteries!

Great Mother Isis
I call you with the vulture's cry
I sing you with the hawk's keen
I embrace you with the vibrating hum
Of the rising bennu phoenix

I die and am reborn
As Ra rises and sets
Traveling the dark hells of amenta
Reborn to rise again as Heru
A shining disc of gold in the East
Fill me with the inner psychic power
May I see the hidden mysteries!

You remain ever constant
In the center of the whirling cosmos
The keeper of the sacred times
The guide of death momentary
And life everlasting.

I call upon you
Mother of magick and mystery
Keeper of the tomb's keys
Revealer of the mysteries of the temple
Mistress of all deep secrets and hidden powers
Come and bless me
Fill me with the power of the throne
The invisible seat of infinite power within
The root of all stability and change.

I am strong and joyous
With you, great Isis,
I am mournful and sorrowful
With you, great Isis,
I am magickal and mysterious
With you, great Isis,
I am loving and transcendent
With you, great Isis.

Let me speak the words of power
That the great work may begin,
Let me dwell in the sacred halls
Anointed with the perfume of Maati—truth.
With bells and incense and sweet wine and desire

I bring you fourth and call you down
Alight as a butterfly great Isis.
A beam of light from a distant star
A lover, a mother, a crone
A dancing veiled vision of all life
Fill me with the inner psychic power.
May I see the hidden mysteries!
Ast urt-hekauti!
Tua ast!

Hail great Isis!
With the uplifting of wings and voices
The opening of the way is begun.
Let all respect all
With divine and balanced love and will
As the word of Maat which shines
As the sun disc upon your brow banishes ego darkness
As the star of your ka illuminates our hearts
As your shining breath banishes all poisons
Together we become one.
Living together through the mysteries of life and death
Laughing and loving together in the inner shrine
Gently filled with the energy of nature
Hail to you great shining one
Coming forth by day and by night
At sunset and sunrise
Gather me as light, as a constellation
Fill me with the inner psychic power
May I see the hidden mysteries!
That I may forever be
Infinite stars in infinite space
Behold Isis! Astu ast!

Goddess Isis Visualization Exercise

You are in a forested clearing by a river
Surrounded by reeds and lotus buds,
You are lying in a large carved stone coffin.
You feel tired, numb, and lifeless,
You can see a veiled figure seated on a throne,
The throne is a large gray stone sphinx.
The old woman is crying
Behind her the dark blue river flows
She is dressed in black and gray.
About her head is a serpent crown
In her right hand is an ankh: a looped cross.
She cries over the sarcophagus with you in it.
She looks into the river,
You smell the river,
You feel the damp breeze,
She gestures and you arise.
She stands and begins to walk west
You follow her as she wanders away.
She suddenly stoops and reaches into the mud.
Rising, you see a star sapphire in her hands.
She smiles at you,
Her eyes are stars,
Her mouth a shadowy red rose.
She places the star sapphire on your left foot,
It is absorbed by your gray flesh.
Suddenly it tingles.
You feel great energy and life come into your foot.
Your psychic powers awake!
Now silently she turns into the forest,
Searching always searching.
In a tree she finds another sapphire.
This is placed on and is absorbed by your right foot;
Your foot comes alive filled with feeling and power.

Your psychic powers awake!
Soon she leaves the forest and treads through a swamp.
Here she finds another jewel;
And this time it is your left leg.
Again it comes alive.
Your psychic powers awake!
And so as you follow this goddess,
She keeps finding jewels,
Touching them to your body,
Bringing you back to life.
With each touch,
Your psychic powers awake!
Now she is in the desert
And the jewel reawakens your right leg.
Now she is in the canyon
And the jewel reawakens your right thigh.
Now she is on the mesa
And the jewel reawakens your left thigh.
Now she is on the beach
And the jewel reawakens your torso.
Now she is in the tundra
And the jewel reawakens your right hand.
Now she is in the arctic
And the jewel reawakens your left hand.
Now she is in the savanna
And the jewel reawakens your right arm.
Now she is in the marsh
And the jewel reawakens your left arm.
Now she is in the rain forest
And the jewel reawakens your right shoulder.
Now she is in the foothills
And the jewel reawakens your left shoulder.
Now she is in the mountains
And the jewel reawakens your neck.
Now she is in the high peaks
And the jewel reawakens your head.

Your psychic powers *awake!*
Now she is in the sky filled with stars,
Stars in her hair and in her eyes,
Hair blowing wildly.
She plucks a jewel from the heavens,
It is a glowing star,
And the jewel reawakens your loins.
This is her final gift,
The shakti power of your body.
Your whole being is alive with energy and awake powers.
You feel reborn and are glowing with a blue light.
The goddess tears off her black robes,
She pulls off her veil.
Her gown is a shimmering peacock green-purple.
She flings the serpent crown from her;
She replaces this with a shining crown
Formed of cow horns and a golden sun disc.
She smiles and takes your hand.
She pulls you toward her.
You begin to dance in the air together,
Laughing and singing,
You spiral down together until you touch the earth.
You touch the earth and flowers grow.
You touch a dead tree and it grows new leaves.
Isis smiles and kisses you.
She sits down upon her sphinx throne,
And the reeds grow up and cover her.
Then the scene fades away . . .

THE GRAND EMPOWERMENT RITUAL OF ISIS: OPENING THE INNER GATES OF PERSONAL POWER AND INNER SIGHT

This ritual will prepare, banish, consecrate and empower you and your "sacred space" toward psychic growth. It enables you to part the veil of past and future so you can see well with your inner sight. It is great for charging up your fortune-telling spot, meditation room, or to prepare an area for psychic development work! Isis is a protective and powerful goddess who personifies the throne of centering, bringing together, and harmony.

You Will Need

◉ a large white stone or crystal

◉ some red wine, fruit, and red flowers, as you like

◉ a vessel of fresh water

◉ matches

◉ natural incense

◉ a red candle

◉ a few reeds or stalks of grass bound together

◉ a marker pen or crayon that will draw on stone

◉ a knife

The Ritual

Do this rite in a comfortable place, either inside or outside.

Enter the sacred place and "part the veil" (arms thrown wide open), facing west, saying:

> Ast un nefer!
> Great mother of all the gods and goddesses
> Root of all life and death
> You who manifest nature
> Open, O Isis, the magick gate
> Reveal the mysteries
> Establish the sacred temple between two rivers
> Between the white and black pillars
> Between the ocean of stars and of tears

Between the inhalation of first breath
And the exhalation of last sigh
From between your thighs, great Mother,
All comes forth and all returns
I am Isis and I come forth!
Nuk ast per kua!

Circle the area and finish in the center, saying:

Maat ert ast netert nefer ker pu setem ankh ua semes ki

Find the center of your area and place the white stone upon it. Everything else is set about the stone with many flowers.

Touch the center of the stone with the reeds or grasses, saying:

Hra then em kher her-a uat!
The face of the queen of heaven bends down
To kiss the earth with brilliance
Tua Ast!
So the temple of Isis is established between the horizons
So the power of Ra the sun and Khonsu the moon
And Sept the holy seven-pointed star
Descends now to bless and empower this sacred place
May my powers awaken! May my inner eye open! Isa make it so!

Toss water to the four directions, each time saying:

Great Mother Isis
Incarnate here as holy earth
May the four goddesses protect my limbs
May my powers awaken! May my inner eye open! Isa make it so!
Sa en hau-k!

Pour some water on the white stone. Light the candle and incense and say:

Hail queen of heaven
You who come forth from all directions at once
And who reside always here in the center
Ruler of magick and mystery
Isis!
Mighty are your enchantments

You embody the words of power
Hidden souls praise the mystery of you,
You reveal the mysteries of the starry sky
Isis!
May my powers awaken! May my inner eye open! Isa make it so!
Isis!

Take up the grasses or reeds and touch them to your four limbs, third eye, two breasts, and sex, chanting the following. As you utter these secret names of Isis, you will become her!

Isa!
By your sacred names I become you and am empowered by you!
May my powers awaken!
May my inner eye open!
Isa make it so!

Khut: mother of the sacred flood
Come forth and part the veil
My powers awaken, my inner eye opens!
Heka en ast!

Usert: earth mother divine
Come forth and part the veil
My powers awaken, my inner eye opens!
Heka en ast!

Satis: great primal fountain of power
Come forth and part the veil
My powers awaken, my inner eye opens!
Heka en ast!

Anquet: Goddess who makes the land to be fertile
Come forth and part the veil
My powers awaken, my inner eye opens!
Heka en ast!

Ankhat: giver of the breath of life
Come forth and part the veil

My powers awaken, my inner eye opens!
Heka en ast!

Renenet: great Mother of the harvest
Come forth and part the veil
My powers awaken, my inner eye opens!
Heka en ast!

Tcheft: great power who feeds her children
Come forth and part the veil
My powers awaken, my inner eye opens!
Heka en ast!

Ament: Goddess of magick who rules the underworld
Come forth and part the veil
My powers awaken, my inner eye opens!
Heka en ast!

In the center, sit before the stone. You are the great mother Isis seated upon the throne-shrine clothed in red with vulture wings. Your shining headdress has horns and a sun disc with a feather in the center. Your pulse is synchronous with the beat of the earth. You are Isis, the mystery of the universe incarnate!

Now, draw an inspired symbol of your inner power on the white stone with the pen or crayon. If none comes to you, then draw the thet or ankh.

When done, feel the power of Isis withdraw inside of you as well as inside the stone. When you are back to being "you," pick up the knife and turn around slowly, counterclockwise, pointing it away from you. Say:

Isis repel and banish all evil!
Khesef khet hem hat met!

When done, offer what is appealing to Isis (flowers, wine, cakes, and so on). Feast and rejoice, saying:

Hail Mother of all gods and men
The sacred place amidst the chaos of Set is firm
And I rejoice within your blessed garden
Grant me wisdom and knowledge and truth

Fill me with love and joy and excitement
Let me be your child
As your one heart
And to be revealed the mysteries
Tua Ast
Hail Isis
Hen-a!

Now blow out the candle and pick up your belongings. Isis remains within you, and you can tap into your psychic powers at any time!

THE GODDESS Kali

ORIGIN: Hindu
ATTRIBUTE: banishing and psychic protection
COLOR: black
SYMBOL: kali yantra (inverted triangle glyph)
ELEMENT: water
STONE/METAL: bone
SCENT: musk or dragon's blood

INTRODUCTION

It could easily be argued that Kali is one of the world's oldest, continually worshipped goddesses. This is appropriate in that her name means "time." It also, quite significantly, means "black," and this is the image of her that is the most commonly found. Though Kali has a fearsome side, she is the protector and destroyer of the shadows within and about us that cause harm and pain. We call upon Kali Ma ("Great Mother") to use her great power to banish negative energies and eliminate things that need to go. Call upon her for a clean start, or a casting-off of unneeded neuroses and problems. She is also said to be the great protectress and giver of wealth. Love that Kali!

Kali is depicted in literally millions of forms. In fact, all Tantrik and

Hindu goddesses are said to be her; the myths abound. She has saved the gods more than once from their enemies, the Asuras. She is said to be all-powerful and her roots are primal.

The Goddess Kali has many masks: Durga, Ma, Bhadra Kali, Shashan Kali, Tara, Lakshmi, Lalita, Bala, Gauri, Devi, Shakti—in fact all facets of Shakti or divine energy in manifestation. Sometime she is shown with her black body being the night sky, filled with stars.

In her most common form she is usually naked or dressed with severed arms and heads. She is beautiful and horrible at the same time, with a long tongue, bloody mouth, fangs, and burning eyes. She variably holds cups of blood, smiling severed heads, axes, swords, spears, mala-beads, and, sometimes even her own severed head. She holds her hands out, blessing her devotees with her hand raised up while banishing all fear, or holds out her hand in the gesture of giving boons. She is always wild, the embodiment of total freedom and liberation, of ego-death and release from illusion and idiocy. She dances to a kind of ultimate rock and roll, the atoms forming and dissolving, the explosions and births that form galaxies, the playing and flowing of particles and waves. It is no coincidence that we are said to be deeply into the Age of Kali, according to Hindus and Tantriks. She embodies all of these things and encodes in her mantras and signs that she unites all of these contradictions; she releases us from duality, warring, and fear. From her even the most loathsome entities flee, because she is the ultimate black hole, the mother to the gate in and out of life and death.

As the earth mother, she teaches us the way to confront and banish our fears and horrors. Life is not always sweet and nice; there is much blood and pain and sorrow. Devotion to Kali Ma lifts us from this mire in realizing and embracing all of these things as part of the mystery and learning of life. Letting go, releasing, cutting free—without these things we could not eat, sleep, make love, or think rationally. She dances through every cleaning, uncluttering, and ending we live through.

Here is a story. Long ago Kali became enraged and began to destroy the universe. The gods could not fight her and fled, sending the God Shiva, Kali's mate, to resist her. He changed into every aspect he could think of but she destroyed every one until finally, as she was on the verge of finishing off the universe, he became inspired. Shiva turned into a helpless infant, and Kali was stopped in her tracks. She completely forgot about destroying and began mothering and protecting. Indeed, this shows great insight into her true character and how we should approach her.

May Kali release us all from our problems, worries, pains, and all that holds us back from being the stars we are! May she release us from all sorrow, revealing the calm center of stillness, and freedom from fear. May she always help us banish and cast off all that attacks or bothers us! Jai Kali!

* * * * *

ℐNVOCATION OF THE GODDESS KALI

Great black mother of all
Goddess of creation and destruction
Mistress of time
Kali Ma, I call you
Come and dance with us
Help us banish and eliminate
All that hinders and hurts!
Jai Kali Ma!

Black hair flying
Krim krim krim
Bells on her ankles ringing
Krim krim krim
Bloody sword is flailing
Krim krim krim
Wide mouth is laughing
Krim krim krim
Holding severed smiling head
Krim krim krim
Hand held up, dispelling fear
Krim krim krim
Hand held out, offering bliss
Krim krim krim
Eyes burning with the flame
Krim krim krim

Body naked filled with stars
Krim krim krim
Necklace of skulls glowing
Krim krim krim
Drums beating her rhythm
Krim krim krim
She dances as thunder
Krim krim krim
Bodies pile up around her
Krim krim krim
Corpses buried and burning
Krim krim krim
Corpses filling the river
Krim krim krim
Cadavers bleeding in streets
Krim krim krim
Dying in silence
Krim krim krim
She gathers the souls in welcoming arms
Krim krim krim
Comforting and caring
Krim krim krim
Smashing their bodies
Krim krim krim
Howling and laughing
Krim krim krim.

Great Kali Ma mother
Mistress of endings and release
Goddess of endings and mother of peace
I call you by the pain I feel
By the chains that bind
By the demons that harass me.
Mother of bones and earth
As death forms within life
Rebirth within horror
So free me from restrictions!

Repel and vanquish all evil!
Banish and purify!

Blast blast
The ignorant and evildoers
Cut cut
Ignorance and blindness
Halt halt
Problems and pain
Put to flight put to flight
All who torture and fight.

Great Kali dancing
Dancing on in my heart
Krim krim krim

Holy mother full of stars
Covering me
Hum hum.

Loving mother suckling
Suckling me
Hrim hrim.

Wild mother laughing
Cleansing me
Of all negativity
Dakshinee Kalikee!

Kali, I call you
I am your child
Terrified and loving and helpless.
Hold us and protect us and banish evil,
Teach us and show us,
Reveal to us the secrets
Of freedom from attachment and fear
That lie in the heart of your darkness.
From you come all things
To you go all things

Mother primal
Time and tide and infinity
I find you here
Deep inside me.

May I banish evil!
May I banish fear
May I banish suffering!
And so fear nothing
In the warm protection
Of your loving arms.

Jai Kali!
Jai Kali!
Jai Kali!

* * * * *

Goddess Kali Visualization Exercise

A skull is in front of you.
You are staring into its eyes,
Into the deep black recesses,
The whirling pools of ink,
And you fall into the blackness.
And you see a figure of black
Forming from the void,
A beautiful naked woman,
Body shining, moving, dancing,
Fangs and lolling tongue,
Bones about her neck and waist.
She holds a skull cup and smiles.
She shows you the inside of her chalice.
There you see dead bodies and ideas,
Burning, rotting, dissolving.
Children, men, women, animals,
Feelings, relationships, ideas, thoughts, dreams,
All dead, all empty, all ashes,

And the ashes fill her cup.
And the blood fills her cup.
And the earth and tears fill her cup.
And she suddenly drinks it,
And is filled with glowing light.
And the light pulses in her,
And her belly glows,
And she begins to dance.
The dance banishes the pain and horror of death.
The dance banishes the peace and release of death.
The dance banishes the inevitable progress of time.
The dance shows the ending of all things.
The dance communicates the letting go,
The releasing of shadows,
Attachments,
Old hurts and angers.
And the dance slows,
And the darkness turns to a light gray.
And now the dance shows people waking up,
Consciousness and kindness spreading
From person to person
Like water from pool to pool.
And the dance fills you with peace.
It fills you with an acceptance of endings,
With an acceptance of the cycles.
And the sun rises.
And she is now dancing in the sun,
And Kali smiles at you,
Black hair flying,
Sharp teeth showing.
And with a gesture
She shows you that you are a part of the cycle
Of birth and death,
Pain and joy.
You see that every action in your life
Is a part of the dance of Kali,

Creating echoes and reverberations
That last forever on the earth,
Vibrating out into the universe.
And the dance slows
And she is now fully pregnant.
And, laughing, she gives birth
To a shining powerful light,
The sun flaring in all directions.
She births a diamond of perfect beauty.
This diamond she offers to you.
Now she transforms into a beautiful woman,
Young, supple, and full of loving laughter.
She dances away,
Merging with the darkness.
The sun sets
And the light becomes gray,
And then becomes black again.
And the beauty of the cycle remains with you,
Dancing with love
In your heart,
Showing you the way
Of letting go.

* * * * *

GRAND EMPOWERMENT RITUAL OF KALI: THE JOY OF BANISHING AND RELEASING

This ritual is to banish any negative energy and make it possible to move on in a positive manner. This ritual should be performed in a graveyard or some very shadowy place at new moon. If you must do this inside, do it in a cellar or very dark room with emblems of death and release about you.

You Will Need

◎ three chicken bones
◎ one found stone

- ⊚ sandalwood incense
  - ⊚ red flowers
    - ⊚ fruit
- ⊚ an image of Kali
  - ⊚ matches
- ⊚ a black candle
  - ⊚ wine

The Ritual

Hold the bones together. Thrust these to the South, North, East, and West, saying each time:

> *Ka li*
> *Put to flight put to flight*
> *All demons and spirits*
> *Who'd hinder this rite!*
> *Phudt!*

And at the center grasp the bones, point them upright, and say:

> *Shi-va*
> *So be it here*
> *Let the vision*
> *Become clear*
> *Ommmmmmmmmmmmmm*

Separate the bones and cast a circle by shaking the bones and walking the circumference of it, saying:

> *Hrim srim krim*
> *Let the circle ring*
> *Hrim srim krim*
> *Let the circle sing*
> *Hrim srim krim*
> *Let the circle bring*

Now place the bones on the ground forming a triangle reversed on the ground. Place the stone in the center. Place the incense, candle, flowers, and fruit before the image of Kali. Light the incense and candle, sit, and meditate on Kali: pure darkness, the inevitability of time, the force of letting go, the mother who takes away what you need to be gone and banishes all evil! After awhile, pour out a small amount of wine to the South, saying:

> *In darkness we honor the ancestors*
> *Bring blessings and understanding*
> *Tarpayami namah!*

Pour out a small amount of wine to the North, saying:

> *In darkness we honor the Earthspirit*
> *Bring blessings and understanding*
> *Tarpayami namah!*

Pour out a small amount of wine to the East, saying:

> *In darkness we honor the stars*
> *Bring blessings and understanding*
> *Tarpayami namah!*

Pour out a small amount of wine to the West, saying:

> *In darkness we honor the elementals*
> *Bring blessings and understanding*
> *Tarpayami namah!*

Pour out a small amount of wine to the center, saying:

> *In darkness we honor the guru ma*
> *The secret self*
> *The great teacher*
> *Great digambara*
> *Kali!*
> *Bring blessings and understanding*
> *Tarpayami namah!*

Meditate upon the womb of the mother before you. Offer Kali what you have brought by placing and pouring it on the stone. See the great black goddess rise up from the earth and dance upon the stone in the center. She has a bloody mouth and star-filled body. She wears a necklace of severed heads. She is laughing and treading upon a corpse, and the corpse is you!

Now stand, with your hands together before you, and say:

> *Kali Kali Kali*
> *Someday I will die*

Kali Kali Kali
Time will take my life
Kali Kali Kali
I will someday be forgotten
Kali Kali Kali
My body will burn to ashes
Kali Kali Kali
I will become free
Kali Kali Kali
Because of your dance
Kali Kali Kali
I confront my death
Kali Kali Kali
I embrace the ending
Kali Kali Kali
We fear the cycle
Kali Kali Kali
Of death and rebirth
Kali Kali Kali
Release us from fear
Kali Kali Kali
Dispel all sorrow
Kali Kali Kali
Letting go of the fear
Kali Kali Kali
We hold life sacred
Kali Kali Kali
Honoring release
Kali Kali Kali
We celebrate freedom
Kali Kali Kali
For every pain a joy
Kali Kali Kali
For every ending, a new life
Kali Kali Kali
We are your sacred cycle

Kali Kali Kali
And so become free
Kali Kali Kali

Clap at each phrase, saying:
May ghosts clinging to life be released
May the ignorant clinging to pain be released
May the suffering and tortured be released
May those seeking peace be released
May we live fully and die beautifully
So we accept our nonexistence now
Becoming the mirror of understanding
Kali Kali Kali
I am that
Tat tvam asi
Om

Now, drink the wine, eat the fruit, smell the flowers, feel the earth:
Become Kali! Pick up the center stone and hold it to your heart. Feel the
black flame of Kali cover and fill you. Your skin is black! Your mouth is
full of sharp teeth! A necklace of skulls is about your neck, you dance
naked amidst the dead! Your enemies scatter before you!

Stand now and begin to sway as you become Kali, as all your attach-
ments, problems, pains, and fears fly away, banished by Ma! Say:
I am Kali Ma
I am the sacred seed-sound Krim
Threefold mother
I am the form and force
Gate of ingress and egress
Focus and axis
About which the wheel turns
I am release!
I am the darkest darkness
And the star shining within it
I am the letting go of that which wounds
And so am the one who loves and heals
I am the destroyer and devourer of evildoers!

I am the protector of children and families!
I am the goddess of death and time!
And the goddess of mercy and compassion!
I am the primal
The root
The deepest power
I am Kali Ma!

Now dance! Dance the dance that destroys and releases all guilt and fear and pain and sorrow! Dance until you are pure motion and pure darkness filled with stars and pure goddess! When the dance of Kali is done, collapse and meditate until you are down again and have returned to being "you." While pouring out the rest of the wine, say:

Honor to the mother
Honor to the teacher
Honor to the initiator
Bhadra Kali, Digambara, Smashan Kali
I receive your teaching with joy
Jai Kali!

Throw the bones and then the stone up and out of the circle, saying:
Return great spirits
Gods, ancestors, and gurus
To the four sacred mountains
There to protect me
And grant me wisdom
As I dwell here in freedom and clarity!
Svaha!

Touch your finger to your lips and see Kali in your heart. Say:
Kali Ma
Stay within
Forever teaching me
To be free
Krim

Stamp the energy into the ground in a counterclockwise circle, saying:

> *Into the earth*
> *Into the ground*
> *Where light and air*
> *Are never found*
> *Into the earth*
> *Into the space*
> *All energy gone*
> *Without a trace*
> *Svaha!*

Now leave the offerings, and depart in peace.

THE GODDESS
Kwan Yin

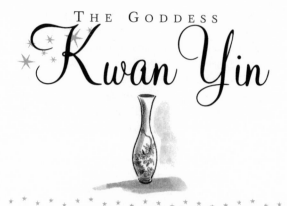

* * * * * * * * * * * * * * * * * * *

ORIGIN: Chinese
ATTRIBUTES: peace and tranquillity
COLOR: white
SYMBOL: a small narrow-necked vase or a dragon
ELEMENT: air
STONE/METAL: pearl
SCENT: any ocean scents or pine

* * * * * * * * * * * * * * * * * * *

INTRODUCTION

Need a little peace and tranquillity in your hectic life? You *know* you do! If so, call upon the beautiful and peaceful goddess Kwan Yin.

Kwan Yin's origins are traced to China, but she was long ago worshipped under other names (like Kannon in Japan) as one of the most venerated and popular goddesses in Asia. She is one of the most widely worshipped goddesses on the planet, under many different names, but she is always considered the goddess of peace and compassion. She is said to be the feminized form of Avalokitesvara, the Buddhist bodhisattva of mercy.

Yet she is also said to have once been a human woman named Myoin in China. She was transformed, and her new name was Kwan Yin. She was also called goddess with a thousand eyes and a thousand arms embracing the earth. It is safe to say that Kwan Yin is a primal mother goddess, probably also a heavenly star who was adopted by Buddhism. She is almost always seen standing on an open lotus.

Aside from her thousand-eyed form she is also sometimes depicted with many faces, but her most common form is as a beautiful woman with black hair, wearing white flowing robes and carrying a slender vase and sometimes a lotus. She is a primal form of the Taoist feminine force of nature, yin—thus her name.

She is often depicted flying over water or rising on a lotus above the raging sea. This relates to her reputation for saving sailors and all people in peril quickly and benevolently. The ocean is the ultimate symbol of yin or feminine energy and is seen as her home.

Whatever her myths, her followers are legion, and her statues can be seen in virtually every temple and park in China. It is common to see statues of her near schools, playgrounds, and maternity hospitals all over Asia in the form of chanting one of her two key mantras: *guan shi yin pu sa* means "honor to the great goddess Kwan Yin"; or *om ma ni bei me hom,* which means "the jewel in the center of the lotus." She is said to dispel all danger and bring peace to the worshipper. Today she is still a very popular goddess, and with very good reason. We all need peace more than ever before.

★ ★ ★ ★ ★

*I*NVOCATION OF THE GODDESS KWAN YIN

From the primal waters
All things are born.

From the earliest point of time
The beginning point of light
Blooming from the churning ocean of space
As a brilliant white lotus
Rising from the limitless depth
The Goddess Kwan Yin
Beautiful
Glowing

Love and peace and wisdom
As it was in the beginning
So we call to her now
Kwan Yin: Bring me peace and tranquillity!
Mother of limitless compassion and love
Throw open the gates of the inner mind,
Fill our every waking moment
With the jasmine scent of your radiance.
Valley spirit,
Primal yin mother
Reveal to us the hidden workings of your mysteries,
Show us the web of life
The chalice, the grail, the cauldron
Of life and death and life again
Kwan Yin: Bring me peace and tranquillity!
The energy connections between all living things
May calm be the elixir
Within the flask you offer
The essence of life
The wisdom of compassion
And we receive now
One sparkling drop
By your hand
From the vase of white jade
Kwan Yin: Bring me peace and tranquillity!
In your other hand
You reveal the white lotus
The basic pattern of all life
Your compassion, knowledge, and wisdom
Cause us to evolve.
You, savioress
The priestess of the endless seas
Emanating love and compassion
From your sacred island paradise p'o t'o.
Rescuer of all who call you,
You descend from the heavens

In a shining golden ray of light
Stars and comets falling with you,
A rainbow filling all of the sky
Lost and distressed
I call you
Kwan Yin: Bring me peace and tranquillity!
And suddenly
I am surrounded by peace
And clarity of vision
And wonder at the beauty
And awe at the complexity
And joy with the consciousness
That I too am part of all.

Again you offer your vessel of power
A vision of pure peace
And absolute tranquillity
A ray of white pours forth
From the opening of the glowing vase
Filling us with light
Transforming and purifying
Eliminating all illness
Bringing peace!

A ray of red pours forth
Filling us with fire
Transforming and purifying
Eliminating all gross attachments.

A ray of blue pours forth
Filling us with equipoise
Transforming and purifying
Eliminating all negative karma
Washing the self clean
Leaving the shining star
Of consciousness.

I receive your love Kwan Yin
Guan shi yin pu sa
I am filled with your alchemy
Guan shi yin pu sa
I become pure consciousness with you
Guan shi yin pu sa
And so become aware
Of the ocean of life
Of which you are the glowing heart.

Beautiful goddess
Standing upon the dragon
You who nurture and help to grow
Become a shining pearl in our hearts
I accept your peace!
As the lotus accepts the bee
As the oyster forms the pearl
Take me
To the island of immortality
The center of calm
The jewel in the center of the lotus
Kwan Yin: Bring me peace and tranquillity!
Guan shi yin pu sa
So ha!

★ ★ ★ ★ ★

GODDESS KWAN YIN VISUALIZATION EXERCISE

Before you, the ocean—
Mighty, deep, dark green.
The scent of the salt comes to you,
The sound of the gulls,
The sight of sun glittering off the waves,
Sandy beaches and cliffs,
Reeds and gnarled trees.
Whales break the surface and crash back down.
Thousands of kinds of fish

Flicker and flash in the depths.
All is in motion.
All is alive.
All is interconnected.
All is at peace.
You turn to your left.
There is a deep primal forest,
Moss hanging from giant trees.
Thousands of kinds of birds
Flutter and flash through the canopy.
Sun filters down in stripes and streaks.
All is interconnected.
All is at peace.
You turn to your left again.
There is a cliff;
You are upon the summit.
Snow sprinkles the rocky ground,
Heather and alpine flowers are around you.
You look out over a vast empty mountain range.
Hawks and eagles circle in the blue sky.
Several very white clouds scuttle by.
Seeds are blown past on tiny fluffs.
The air is cool and sharp and sweet.
All is at peace.
You turn to the left again.
The cliff fades into a desert.
The sun full overhead is hot.
The rippled sands glare in the noonday sun.
Vultures hop across a dune and take off.
The burning scent of sage fills the air
As the heat shimmers over the ground.
All is at peace.
You turn to the left for the last time.
You are staring at the ocean again,
Every living thing connected
With every other living thing,

All at peace.
You are in the center of this vast matrix.
You are part of it.
In the center of this vast peace you see a lotus.
It opens . . . there!
Kwan Yin, the primal goddess.
She is holding before her a shining pearl.
It is the source of all life.
It shines pure peace . . . all is peace.
You look carefully,
And you can see the glimmer of Kwan Yin's peace
Flickering off every tree, animal, rock, and wave.
And this light of peace fills you,
And Kwan Yin is in your heart.
You are all life.
You are peace.

★ ★ ★ ★ ★

GODDESS EMPOWERMENT RITUAL OF KWAN YIN: RECEIVING THE PEACE OF KWAN YIN

This is a ritual of connecting with the earth and all the natural healing power of the planet as the living personification of peace and tranquillity. To become Kwan Yin is to become the compassion of the planet, the very spirit of peace. Be sure to collect the necessary objects for this spell from your own neighborhood.

You Will Need
◉ a rattle
◉ a bone
◉ a feather
◉ a seed
◉ water from an outside tap or, better yet, a body of water
◉ a small spade or trowel

The Ritual

The place of power for the rite should be near the ocean or other body of water. An island is best. If you must do this inside, have a large basin of water before you or even do the rite in a bathtub full of water!

Walk around in a circle, shake the rattle eight times, and say:

> *Thunder, lightning*
> *Sun, moon, and fire*
> *Wind and rain*
> *Ocean's desire*
> *Cleanse and clean*
> *Sweep away*
> *Filth and error*
> *All night and day!*
> *So ha!*

Slow the beat of the rattle and cast a circle clockwise, saying:

> *Om ma ni bei me hom!*
> *Peace, peace, peace.*

Shake the rattle above the items assembled and say:

> *Mother, center, open, earth*
> *Kwan Yin*
> *Goddess*
> *Bless and empower me*
> *Bring forth the primal yin*
> *Meeting the dragon*
> *The primal yang*
> *Vessel of Teh*
> *Bring forth the knowing of Tao*
> *That I may become peace!*
> *Open the eye*
> *The heart*
> *The root*
> *To full tranquillity*
>
> *I will now*
> *To remember the peace of my beginnings*

> *Uniting once again*
> *Awareness and calm*
> *Within the web of all living things*

Take up the bone and touch all of your body, saying:

> *Joy of life*
> *Locked in root of flesh*
> *Make me one Kwan Yin*
> *With animal consciousness*
> *That I may become the calm and innocence*
> *Of the living fauna about me*

Walk around in a circle, and shake the rattle eight times. Say:

> *Kwan Yin shi pu sa.*

Take up the feather and touch your body, saying:

> *Breath of life*
> *Wings of light*
> *Make me one Kwan Yin*
> *With aerial consciousness*
> *That I may become the calm and joy*
> *Of the living winged ones about me*

Take up the seed and touch all of your the body, saying:

> *Green of life*
> *In root of leaf and vine*
> *Make me one Kwan Yin*
> *With plant consciousness*
> *That I may become the calm and beauty*
> *Of the living flora about me*

Take up the water and touch all the body:

> *Water of life*
> *In root of liquid*
> *Make me one Kwan Yin*
> *With sea life consciousness*
> *That I may become the calm and bliss*
> *Of the living water beings about me*

Lie down with the bone in the right hand, seed in the left, feather at your feet, and water at your head.

Place the flower on your chest and say:

>*Om ma ni bei me hom*
>
>*I am Kwan Yin!*
>
>*Mother and consciousness of all*
>
>*Gone is ego and separateness!*
>
>*Gone is restriction!*
>
>*Gone blindness to peace, innocence, joy, beauty, and bliss!*
>
>*Guan shi yin pu sa!*
>
>*Om!*
>
>*I am peace! I am innocence! I am joy! I am beauty! I am bliss!*
>
>*Om!*

Open yourself to the ecosystem. Systematically relax each part of your body. Extend your energy into the earth, the sky, and the sea. Feel your aura and consciousness move with every plant, animal, insect and microbe. Feel the web of life fill your mind with utter peace and tranquillity! Feel it become your body. Feel your heart beating with all hearts to one clear beat. When you have this beat take up the rattle and shake it to the beat! You are Kwan Yin, source of the pulse of all life, center of peace! Visualize every living thing while chanting:

>*I am that . . . I am that . . . I am that . . .*

Finish:

>*I am that; I am all*
>
>*With all I rise*
>
>*With all I fall*
>
>*Life and death*
>
>*Night and day*
>
>*Pain and pleasure*
>
>*Ever-changing play*
>
>*In the center of all*
>
>*Is great release*
>
>*I am center of all*
>
>I am peace!
>
>*Om ma ni bei me hom!*

When you come back to being "you," and feel completely at peace, finish the ritual by digging a hole with the trowel. Bury all the items except the rattle in the earth.

Shake the rattle above where the items are buried, then throw it in the water, saying:

> Kwan Yin
> Bless and empower this working
> The eye: remember peace
> The heart: remember peace
> The root: remember peace
> That all may awaken peace
> To full knowledge peace
> Uniting once again
> Awareness and knowing
> Within the web of all living things
> As peace
> Om man ni bei me hom!

Then go.

THE GODDESS
Lakshmi

ORIGIN: Hindu
ATTRIBUTE: wealth and prosperity
COLOR: gold or red and green
SYMBOL: shri yantra (Hindu glyph)
ELEMENT: earth
STONE/METAL: gold
SCENT: sandalwood

INTRODUCTION

"Salutations to thee, Maha Maya, abode of fortune,
worshipped by gods, wielder of conch and mace, Maha Lakshmi,
I bow to thee!"

—MAHALAKSHMI ASTAKAM STOTRAM

Lakshmi is in many ways the supreme mother goddess of prosperity. Revered throughout Hinduism as the goddess of blessings and wealth, she is also the primary goddess of security and material comfort. She is often depicted holding a pink lotus and showering her worshippers with golden coins. She is connected with and often shown with the God Ganesh, the elephant-headed Hindu god of removing obstacles and bringing wealth. In the Tantrik trinity of the triple goddess (maiden, mother, crone) Lakshmi is the mother. Today she is usually shown as the wife of the later-evolving God Vishnu, the preserver of the world, but her earlier husband was definitely the God Rudra. He is the red-skinned archetypal wild man, the god of storms and wild animals. He is the howler and ruler of the deep forests and lonely mountains. In fact, he is one of the ancient root gods of the lord Shiva.

The ancient festival of lights in October of which she is a focus also celebrates her union with Shiva. On this night all wives dance for their husbands, invoking Lakshmi and the fortune, prosperity, and success she brings. She is said to have been born when the demons churned the universe and the primal ocean of milk as they struggled with the gods for supremacy. She was born from their chaos and churning, rose from the maelstrom upon a pink lotus, and instantly filled all the gods and demons with happiness.

She is one of the most popular goddesses in India and as such she is worshipped by any and all, especially those in need of material prosperity or nourishment. Her earliest function was surely that of earth mother goddess. As such some of the very ancient images depict her lying down, prominently displaying her yoni and having a lotus flower for a head.

If you go into any Hindu-owned business or company, you will always find an image of Lakshmi or a small shrine to her near the cash register. She is prayed to every day by businessmen and householders to increase profits and bring economic prosperity. Most Hindus believe that she helps them in this way.

She is invoked as beloved goddess MahaLakshmi, and as wisdom mother she is the knower of all, the giver of all boons, a terror to the wicked, and the remover of all sorrows. She is the bestower of intelligence, success, and worldly enjoyment and liberation. Thus she is without beginning or end, primordial energy, goddess of all, and a great power or *shakti*. Always invoked as the goddess seated on a lotus, she is also seen as the creatrix of all in her form of the supreme universal mother.

It is easy to see the universal appeal of this powerful goddess. What makes her so favored by millions is the fact that she is a very practical goddess who brings real tangible prosperity and wealth to her devotees. As such, we call upon her now to help us to bring wealth and prosperity to those in need.

O auspicious one, giver of boons, MahaLakshmi, hear our prayers!
MahaLakshmi namaste!

* * * * *

Goddess Lakshmi Invocation

Greatest Mother
Beautiful and loving
Clothed in red and green
And brightest gold
Crown of gold and jewels
Chains of gold on arms and neck
Bells of gold about your ankles
Shining as the sun.
Bring the gold of prosperity
The gold of money
The gold of happiness and hope.
Greatest blessed goddess
You who are full and powerful,
Mother who loves
And feels for us, her children
Heart full of maternal wisdom
Give us wealth and care
Scatter your blessings as jewels
Upon us who need your help,
Reach down with your perfect hands
And let the arid lands of our poverty grow green,
Dance upon the rivers of life
And bring forth the pink lotus
Of abundance and joy.
We are in dire need,
Fill our home with food
Cover the fields with life
Open the grasping hands
And let great wealth
Freely flow to us who need.

Mother, we call you
A billion hungry voices,
Mother we need you
Mother we beseech you
Let us live in prosperity!
Fill our hands with plenty
Transmit the wisdom of sharing
Bring the joy of fulfillment
Ease all suffering
With your love and your compassion.
You are living here now
Source of all teachings and of all good
You fill the sky
Creatrix of all things
You smash the demons
Of need and poverty
As a lioness riding the power
Of the raging storm.
Great Lakshmi,
We invoke you here now
Fill our arms
With the universal blessings
Grant these simple goals to us now
And to each and every human being
Bring wealth!
Bring wealth!
Bring money!
Bring money!
Bring prosperity!
Bring prosperity!
That your joy may be mirrored
In the chants of universal rejoicing

Om hrim srim Lakshmi namah svaha!

* * * * *

GODDESS LAKSHMI VISUALIZATION EXERCISE

Breathe deeply.
Feel yourself unwind.
Relax each part of your body.
Become aware of the earth as one living being.
You can feel and hear her heartbeat;
It is one with your heartbeat.
Breathe deeply, feel the connection.

Now . . .

A vast milky sea is before you,
Endless and translucent,
The stuff of glowing stars and galaxies,
Gently undulating,
Rippled by a warm and sultry breeze.
The sky is light blue,
Sparkling with gold-tinted clouds
Sunshine is everywhere.

Suddenly there is turbulence
In the center of this glowing sea.
A shaking and swirling,
Churning and spinning,
Until a whirlpool forms,
Growing larger and larger,
More and more intense.
And suddenly
The beautiful goddess Lakshmi emerges,
Parting the milky sea,
Eyes closed,
Beautiful white robes,
Covered in gold and jewels,
Holding a lotus in her left hand
And gold coins in her right.
At her feet is a pot of gold,

And fountains of gold pieces erupt
And shower the sea around her.

She opens her eyes.
They are burning emeralds.
The scents of honey and sandalwood
Fill the air.
She smiles,
And the sky is filled with a bright light.
All is gold.
And she opens her arms,
And the ocean changes
Into a golden field.

She is suddenly standing
Amidst waves of grain,
The sun shining above her.

She smiles again and points with her hand
To the jar at her feet.
It is golden
With a lid
Shaped into the image of an elephant
With red threads
Wrapped around it.

She bends down and picks it up
Nodding her head,
She hands it to you
And gestures behind you.

You open the jar.
Inside are jewels and pieces of gold.
All are for you
And for those you love.

The world is filled
With joyous happy people
Spinning around Lakshmi.

Lakshmi gently hugs you
And whispers
"You have given well,
Now
Look into the bottom of the jar,
For there is a special gift for you."

You look into the jar.
It is there for you.
It is what you *need*.
You take it
And kiss Lakshmi on the cheek,
Uttering your thanks.

Suddenly all the dancers
Flow into whirling liquid
Like milk filled with stars.
Lakshmi dissolves,
Leaving the smell of perfume behind,
And the milky sea is suddenly still again.
And a warm breeze blows
Over the darkening sky.

Now you come back to your body,
You feel the joy and peace of Lakshmi filling all your limbs,
Your torso,
Your heart, and mind.
You feel the earth's heartbeat, and it begins to fade.
You feel this within you
As you breathe deeply, relaxed and refreshed and earthed.

Now awake reenergized and ready for prosperity!

★ ★ ★ ★ ★
Goddess Lakshmi Empowerment Ritual: Becoming the Power of Wealth and Prosperity

Lakshmi, the goddess of wealth and prosperity, can change your life for the better if you accept her empowerment. Doing this empowerment says to the Goddess Lakshmi that you want her to be part of you, to protect, help, empower, and bless you. It is not so much that she will make you wealthy, though she will bring money and material things to you when needed, but she will make you *experience* your life with pleasure and prosperity. Tired of having a "poverty" mentality? Let Lakshmi into your heart and live a better, happier, more fulfilling existence *and* gain the material prosperity you need!

You Will Need
◉ a small pile of sixteen different gold- and/or silver-
colored coins you have collected
◉ a Lakshmi image
◉ matches
◉ sandalwood incense
◉ a yellow or gold candle
◉ yellow flowers
◉ some honey
◉ a gold necklace or medallion dedicated to Lakshmi
◉ sandalwood oil

The Ritual

This should be done at midday—a Sunday is best. You should do it inside or outside in a garden, but you should be alone and undisturbed for at least an hour. And it should be sunny, if possible.

When ready, artfully arrange all the items on a small table or stone altar facing north. Sit, breathe slowly, and relax. Imagine a circle of white light around you, protecting you and banishing all negativity.

Place the coins in a pile before the image of Lakshmi. Light the incense and candle. Place one flower atop the pile of coins and say:

> *Shrim Shrim Shrim*
> *Mother daughter come*
> *Shrim shrim shrim*
> *Shining as the sun*
> *Shrim shrim shrim*
> *Plenty to us all*
> *Shrim shrim shrim*
> *Let the blessings fall*

Close your eyes, eat some of the honey, and touch the flower on the pile of coins, saying:

> *Mother Lakshmi we feel you*
> *Soft and warm and full of life,*
> *Mother Lakshmi we smell you*
> *Fertile and fresh and giving life,*
> *Mother Lakshmi we hear you*
> *Rolling and singing and chanting life,*
> *Mother Lakshmi we taste you*
> *Sweet and sharp and blossoming with life.*

Open your eyes and meditate on the image of Lakshmi.

Put on the necklace dedicated to Lakshmi. Then put some of the oil on the flower atop the coins and on your forehead, heart, and lower belly, saying:

> *Mother Lakshmi we see you*
> *Flesh of our flesh and life of our life.*
>
> *We honor you with love*
> *We honor you with laughter*
> *We honor you with life*
> *Be here—be here—be here—now!*

Repeat eight times:

> *Om hrim srim Lakshmi namah svaha!*

When you feel her presence, stand and throw your hands up and say:

> *Lakshmi Devi*
> *Greatest goddess*

> *By the power of your sacred jewels*
> *With the power of your sacred flower*
> *Through the power of your blessed wealth*
> *Splash the milk-white ocean of your prosperity*
> *Upon my life and body,*
> *Fill me with your life*
> *That I may bring forth and embody*
> *Plenty and joy and peace*
> *For myself, my loved ones, and for all I encounter.*
> *Om! Greatest goddess born of union*
> *Mother of the universe*
> *Body of prosperity*
> *You are me—you are me—you are me—now!*

Now, see yourself, Lakshmi, goddess of wealth!
Take a coin from the pile and go to the East. Toss it up, saying:

> *Body of the goddess*
> *Fly out to the east*
> *Grant wealth to all living beings there*
> *With your flesh and blood*
> *Lakshmi namah svaha!*

Toss a coin to the South, saying:

> *Body of the goddess*
> *Fly out to the South*
> *Grant wealth to all living beings there*
> *With your flesh and blood*
> *Lakshmi namah svaha!*

Toss a little coin to the West, saying:

> *Body of the goddess*
> *Fly out to the West*
> *Grant wealth to all living beings there*
> *With your flesh and blood*
> *Lakshmi namah svaha!*

Toss a coin to the North, saying:

> *Body of the goddess*

> *Fly out to the North*
> *Grant wealth to all living beings there*
> *With your flesh and blood*
> *Lakshmi namah svaha!*

Place your hands on the pile of coins, as Lakshmi, saying:

> *Mother-earth it!*
> *Make it so*
> *Fill all our fields and homes*
> *With prosperity and wealth.*
> *Fill our pockets*
> *Give to us prosperity*
> *Rain down wealth*
> *Upon all of us who need.*
> *Fill us with the sense of wonder*
> *Bless these seeds of wealth,*
> *Your sleeping children*
> *With the golden spark*
> *Of your power and joy*
> *That your magick wealth*
> *May be spread about the land!*
>
> *Body of the goddess*
> *Be the earth to all who need,*
> *Nourish all living beings now*
> *With your flesh and blood*
> *Lakshmi namah svaha!*

Take a big double handful of the coins and raise them above your head. With eyes closed, let the coins gently fall upon your head and shoulders. In your mind see the golden coins and blessings of Lakshmi fill you and your home, your business, your bank accounts, your life, and the lives of your friends! Feel the golden power of her settle into your body!

The power of Lakshmi is within you now, surrounded by the power of wealth and prosperity. You are gold!

Bow to the goddess three times and say:

> *I am blessed*
> *I am Lakshmi, namaste!*
> *I am filled with your joy*
> *I am Lakshmi, namaste!*
> *I am the embodiment of prosperity*
> *I am Lakshmi, namaste!*
> *I will carry this forever*
> *Into my life*
> *And the lives of all I touch*
> *I am Lakshmi, namaste!*
> *I am health, wealth, prosperity and freedom to all beings*
> *I am the eternal sound* srim!
> *I am Lakshmi, namaste!*
> *Svaha!*

Sit and absorb the loving light of Lakshmi. Feel your blessing spread across the world!

When you return to being "you," blow out the candle, put out the incense, and take off the necklace. Clap your hands three times, then bury three of the coins in the earth somewhere, offering them to Lakshmi.

You must give the rest of the coins as special prosperity love-offerings to friends, family, and charities as well as to those who are in need. Keep only three of these coins in front of the Lakshmi image.

You are now very blessed and empowered by the most excellent Goddess Lakshmi.

THE GODDESS Maat

ORIGIN: Egyptian
ATTRIBUTES: justice and karmic balance
COLOR: violet (ultra!)
SYMBOL: a black feather
ELEMENT: air
STONE/METAL: amethyst
SCENT: aloe or mastic

Introduction

If you have come to a place in your life where you need divine balance, justice, or the supreme light of truth, call upon Maat! She cannot stand to see injustice, and she can help you find the heart of peaceful balance.

The Goddess Maat is an ancient deity of Egypt, where she was worshipped for thousands of years as the personification of truth, balance, and cosmic justice in an ordered universe. She is usually shown with the wings of a vulture, her special animal, and she is often recognized by the feather of truth that crowns her forehead. Many feel that modern images of Justice with a blindfold and scales are latter-day interpretations of Maat.

According to the ancient Egyptians, the Goddess Maat lays out the daily course of the sun across the heavens, and makes the stars, moon, and planets orbit their appointed rounds in the preordained manner commanded by the universe. In fact, she personifies the universe as the force of cosmic balance and harmony. Maat is also called, in various places, Mat, Maet, and Maati. These are different aspects of the same cosmic goddess.

Maat could easily be identified with the Eastern concept of karma in the cosmic balance that was her being extended to the living and dead and all gods and spirits. When a person died, they had to be judged before the lord of the underworld Osiris. This judging was done by weighing their soul (symbolized by a heart) against the feather of truth/Maat. If the two balanced they could enter the blessed abode, but if truth outweighed the heart they were devoured by the monster-god Amit. On a more earthly level, it was Maat who held society together making the flow of power and responsibility balanced and workable.

The pharaoh was said to rule "by Maat." When wars, dynastic struggles, or lawlessness swept across the country, scribes often noted that Maat had left the land. In this sense we can see that Maat is the personification of social balance and interdependence. Thus invoking her is appropriate for righting wrongs and trying to help truth and understanding emerge from any situation.

Egyptian mythology teaches that in the beginning of time, there was a primal ocean, a void of chaos covered with water. At one point a mound of earth arose from the primal flood and so the beginning of land was manifested. This primal mound is often called Maat, and it is sometimes represented as a symbol that also can be read in hieroglyphics as Maat. Thus, invoking Maat brings us back to the primal beginnings of the earth, helps us find common ground, and reinfuses our life and works with balance and truth.

* * * * *

$\mathcal{G}$ODDESS MAAT INVOCATION

Great mother of the Sun
Descend into the arms of the earth
Winged goddess of balance
Come unto me who cry out to you

For justice and truth and strength
Help me find balance in the world!
I call upon you to help balance the energies
In my life,
I call upon you to bring the truth
Into all I do and say and feel,
I call upon you to give me strength,
To persevere on all levels in healing myself
On all levels
In organizing, in uniting
And in bringing a halt to all destruction!
I invoke
The black free-standing feather of Maat
The crystal star gleaming within
The outpouring of interstellar energies
Flowing and snaking through the earth
Filling every living thing
With the will toward harmony
And balance.
I invoke the point of equilibrium
The force of momentum,
Gravity and electron-spin resonance
Filling us with the song
Of balance.
I invoke the law of the universe
The innate justice
That governs all things.
May I channel this energy in my work
May I be a conduit of the black flame of justice
And the silence of truth in action.
May I be unified with all living beings
Through the breath of Maat
And may her heartbeat fill my ears
As the sound of a singing healed life!
O Maat!
Mother of infinity

Goddess who guides the sun,
The planets
And all the ever-moving stars
Guide me now in my hour of need!
Great cosmic mother
May it be so.

Tua Maati!
We invoke the black-haired goddess
Who balances the souls of all beings
Who, weighed with the heart,
Reveals all things.
May I enter the chamber of truth
And stand before the great power of justice.
Maat, crowned with the feather,
Reveal yourself in all your manifestations.
We call forth the center of truth and justice
From within and without
We name this power Maat
And we manifest it here and now
As knowledge, will, and action.
Through the strength and energy of our arms
May the balance of Maat
Be done!
Through the clarity of our minds and loins
May the balance of Maat
Be done!
Through the black flame of justice in my heart
May the balance of Maat
Be done!
Tua Maati!

* * * * *

GODDESS MAAT VISUALIZATION EXERCISE

There is a dark hall before you.
Thousands of shadows flicker there.

Deeper you go into the earth
Until you come to a vast cave.
There is a stone in the center of the cave;
Out of the stone flow four streams,
Each going off into the darkness
Toward each of the four quarters,
And there is a torch of crystal on the stone
And before it is a golden balance.
You reach to your heart
And it appears in your hands
As a ball of light.
You place this
In the left dish of the scales.
Suddenly the torch flame
Becomes black
But still filling the cave
With ultraviolet light.
The flame bends down,
Touching the right dish of the scales,
Becoming a black feather.
Slowly all that you have done in life
Pulses through the glowing heart.
All you have done to better the world,
To heal the earth and other people—
The balance tilts one way,
Then the other.
You see how you are being weighed
Against the universe
Until they balance perfectly.
And you utter the word
Maat.

Suddenly the beautiful goddess
Emerges from the black flame
And appears before you,
Holding the black feather

Within the energy sphere
Of your heart power.
She smiles
And places this within your heart.
And you feel balanced,
One whole and free.
This center of balance
Will fill you forever.
It will guide you in justice.

The glorious goddess stares at you.
Black eyes filled with stars,
A crown with one feather upon it,
And a cape shimmering
With peacock colors.
She throws up her hands,
And suddenly the darkness of the cave
Becomes filled with stars.
You feel fresh air
And smell fresh grass.
You are standing upon a hill
In the wilderness
At night
With the goddess.
She kisses you,
Turns, and walks away into the dunes,
Slowly merging with the Milky Way.
And even then
The stars fade away
And you return with the energies of Maat
To this world.

* * * * *

$\mathcal{G}$ODDESS MAAT EMPOWERMENT RITUAL:
BECOMING THE SPIRIT OF TRUTH,
JUSTICE, AND BALANCE

Maat is the goddess manifesting balance, and so a return to balance is the key to this ritual. The Maat energy helps balance our inner selves as well as the unbalanced energies in our life. The world is within as well as without; the great mother Maat is called upon to energize us, to balance our chi (energy), and to help us find justice, equality, and truth within ourselves and in all our endeavors.

You Will Need
@ black and silver clothes to wear
@ a balance scale or other symbol(s) of balance and justice
@ a large feather
@ matches
@ a white candle
@ a black candle
@ a mysterious incense like musk

The Ritual

Put on the silver and black clothes. Sit alone in a sacred wild space or in a very quiet and peaceful room with a feather and what images or symbols of balance and truth and justice you wish and with any and all tools of magick you feel appropriate. Meditate on what truth, justice, and balance really mean. When ready, say:

> I stand alone
> Upon the sacred stone
> Rising on the hill of creation
> From the broiling sea of chaos
> That surrounds all.

Silently meditate and then say:

> The breath of the divine
> Energy moving through matter
> Becoming: unbecoming

The Ultimate Guide to Goddess Empowerment ★ 176

> *Rearranging all existence*
> *Bringing forth life*

Lift and focus on the feather as you rise, saying:

> *I am I*
> *The worldspirit manifest*
> *Tending toward balance*
> *Patterned in harmony*
> *Spinning in equilibrium*
> *Here then*
> *As truth*
> *I become*
> *The flame of truth*
> *Ipsos!*

Light the candles and incense. Then face the East, holding the feather and saying:

> *I blow as winds of truth*
> *Atmospheric fields of balance*
> *Scattered atoms dancing in harmony*
> *A feather of air.*

Face the South, saying:

> *I burn as tongues of truth*
> *Glowing pools of magma balance*
> *Solar rays alight in harmony*
> *A feather of fire.*

Face the West, saying:

> *I flow as oceans of truth*
> *Pulsing pounding rivers of balance*
> *Lunar cycle-tides in harmony*
> *A feather of water.*

Face the North, saying:

> *I exist as the matter of truth*
> *The life-death physical balance*
> *Hum and spark of the world in harmony*
> *A feather of earth.*

Focus on your heart. Touch the feather to your heart and say:

All of cosmos is self
Self-created
So here is the Great Pattern
The natural Balance
Harsh and beautiful
That we find and are part of
At birth
Maat!

Become the great goddess! Become the cosmic balance, the force of truth, the goddess of justice! Dance slowly in a spiral clockwise out from the center, slowly chanting:

Truth and balance and harmony
All of the world is within me
I am Maat!
I am balance, truth, and justice!
Ipsos!

As you reach the rim of the circle, go slowly and pace about it, saying:

I am the orbit of planets and stars!
I am the path of the sun and moon and earth!
I am the will and love of every life!
Maat!

Pause and then circle again in silence. Circle around the third time pointing with the feather to each of the four directions, saying:

Truth
Balance
Harmony
Feather of Maati
Realign all
In truth and balance
All be free!

Imagine your energy pushing work that helps bring truth, balance, and justice to the world and all you love and care for. Touch the feather to your forehead and feel it burning on your brow. You are Maat!

Return to the center. Simply charge and empower yourself by placing the quill end of the feather on your head, heart, and loins, then circling your body, saying:

> *Truth spirals out*
> *Truth spirals in*
> *Maat a burning fire*
> *Truth now inspire!*

Feel the flow of the black flame of Maat flowing out as a balancing/harmonizing force to everyone. Make your own personal statement of balance, utter your will for truth, or what you see as the optimal future. See it happen.

Now, come back to "you," and let the power of Maat leave you, spreading truth. When you are ready, take up your feather and spiral outward past the edge of your circle, saying:

> *Make it happen*
> *It will be*
> *Love and will and harmony*
> *Maat!*

As you leave the sacred site, throw the Maat energies out, using the sacred feather and your inner sight. When it is scattered, fling the feather out with it, leaving it to fly away, saying:

> *Soar Maat!*
> *In sky and sea*
> *May all be balance*
> *Let it be!*
> *Ipsos!*

Blow out the candles and incense, and dance away into your new life.

THE GODDESS Morrigan

ORIGIN: Celtic
ATTRIBUTES: competition and assertiveness
COLOR: blood red
SYMBOL: sword or crow
ELEMENT: fire
STONE/METAL: iron or steel
SCENT: tobacco or burning wood

INTRODUCTION

Need some aggressive energy in your life? You need a kick-ass goddess like Morrigan. She is the tough warrior goddess who helps you whup butt on the playing field, in the corporate world, and in your personal life. Call her the goddess of personal power!

Morrigan is the greatest goddess figure of old Irish mythology, and her name means "great queen." Later forms include the famous Morgan Le Fay of Arthurian romance, as well as Fata Morgana, the queen of the faerie realms. She has many names and many forms. She frequently appears as a triad, the triple goddess incarnate, or even as a group in ninefold form. This makes her appear stronger to those she must compete against. Her nature, however, is most often dual as a figure of both war and bold sexuality, a taker and a giver of life, and both dark and bright in one form.

She appears most frequently as a goddess of battle, and her alter egos are Macha, "great queen of phantoms"; Nemhain, or "frenzy"; and Badb, which means "crow, raven." The ravens and other carrion birds who congregated over ancient battlefields were often seen as the dark forms or messengers of the goddess. These are similar to the Norse valkyries or battle maidens of Viking myth, who likewise appeared in groups of three or nine.

Morrigan features prominently in the epic tale of Cuchulain, and her archetype survived as queen of the faerie realms, and later as the tragic sister of King Arthur. We call upon her proud and noble energies to make us stronger, tougher, and more self-confident. Truly the way of the warrior is important for each of us in this world today. Morrigan is not only the goddess of destruction and killing; this is only part of her power. She is also the goddess of focused power, protecting the weak, defending those who need it, and defeating oppression, especially against women!

* * * * *

Goddess Morrigan Invocation

Out of the heart of night eternal
And the dark wind of the storm of battle
We call that great and terrible queen
Who is called old Morrigan.

Triple formed as the changing moon,
Lover of heroes and lady of battle,
Who gives birth with love
And fights without mercy.

Mystery transforming
As the waxing and waning moon,
Shape-shifting sorceress
Whose secret is hidden;

Cloaked in crimson
Dark as spilled blood,

Fiery-eyed and beautiful
As the edge of a sharp sword!

You are Nemhain,
The frenzy of battle,
Savage maiden
Who delights in fighting oppression!

You are the Badb,
Black raven flying
Bird of dark omen
Who feasts on the dead
Making way for the new!

You are Macha,
Queen of phantoms,
Mother of spirits
Of the fallen!

Companion of warriors
And inciter of wildness,
Sword stained red,
Eyes bright with lust.

You ride on your black horses
In the form of a multitude of women,
You soar on the storm clouds
As a company of crows!

You live in the blades of sharp weapons
And the spilling of blood,
In the passion of warfare
And the joy of fierce competition!

You are terrible in battle,
Full of power and joy
You are without mercy
In the guarding of the land!

Wild queen of night and fire,
Power of protection
Force and strength
Overcome all opposition!

Great Morrigan,
We invoke you by your names!
Nemhain! Badb! Macha!
Ride with us that we may win!

* * * * *

GODDESS MORRIGAN VISUALIZATION EXERCISE

You are within the green glow of the living earth,
Feeling the sphere of the globe
As the physical extent of your body,
The manifestation of your flesh.
The seas are the flow of your blood,
The mountains are your bones,
The winds your breath.
The roads and cities are your nervous system,
The dreams of humanity your mind.
And throughout this body
There is warfare and destruction,
And there is the making way
For the new life.
There is anger and contention
And there is friendly competition,
The cry of teams and players.
There is negative conflict.
There is positive competition.
In the midst of both
There is crackling energy,
There is the strength,
The power.
The great warrior goddess
Who wears two faces—

It is the goddess who is the world,
It is she who fights in every battle,
Who competes in every race.
And in her rage and frenzy,
Joy and ecstasy,
You sense the defense of the good
And the opposing of evil.
In the ceaseless struggle of the people
Are the birth pangs
Of a better future striving to be born.
In the revolutions are cries for justice,
In the wars are a reaching for peace,
In the violence is a need for self-defense.
In all of this rough play
The mind of the world is striving
For better dreams,
And the heroes strive to defend what they love.
And this is the joy of Morrigan!
For we are all one world,
One life, one flesh;
And life is struggle, competition, and joy
And from that lesson you turn away,
Falling back to where you began,
To breathe in the healing and hope of the world
The energies of strength
And compassion.

* * * * *

$\mathcal{G}$RAND EMPOWERMENT RITUAL OF MORRIGAN: GATHERING OF WARRIOR POWER!

Feel threatened at all? In a rage over injustice? Wish to become the great warrior goddess and avenge wrongs or just win that tennis tournament? Become the Red One and conquer all! This ritual is the gathering of personal power! You will take the three roles of the different aspects of Morrigan. No one will ever push you around again!

You Will Need

- ◎ a red cloth
- ◎ a spear, sword, or knife
- ◎ matches
- ◎ a spicy-scented incense, like cinnamon
- ◎ a red candle
- ◎ red wine
- ◎ an iron cup (if possible)
- ◎ red flowers
- ◎ some berries
- ◎ a crow feather
- ◎ a small spade or trowel
- ◎ an image of Morrigan (warrior goddess)

The Ritual

At midday, dress in red and black leather—warrior garb if possible! In a dry place, on a hill or field if possible, gather all these things together and place them on the red cloth facing the South.

When ready, salute the four directions with your spear, sword, or knife, saying:

> *The call goes forth*
> *To the four corners of the world;*
> *May the warrior power gather*
> *To clothe me in lightning!*
> *Guardians of the four gates,*
> *Summon the ancient powers!*

Light the incense and face the East, saying:

> *By the sword of Nuada do I call*
> *The winds of the eastern gate!*
> *May the blade of battle be upraised*
> *To protect and empower my will!*
> *Badb, bear witness to our rite!*

Light the candle and face the South, saying:

> *By the spear of Lugh do I call*
> *The fires of the southern gate!*
> *Flame and fury, I face the foe,*
> *Beat back oppression and ignorance!*
> *Nemhain, bear witness to our rite!*

Pour the wine into the cup and spill a little on the ground, facing the West, saying:

> *By the cauldron of Daghdha do I call*
> *The waters of the western gate!*
> *The power of the tidal wave*
> *Shall my spirit from attack!*
> *Macha, bear witness to our rite!*

Pierce a flower with your blade, face the North, scatter the berries around you, and say:

> *By the stone of Fal do I call*
> *The living earth of the northern gate!*
> *Flesh of the world and foundation of life,*
> *May I be strong in the war against evil!*
> *Morrigan, bear witness to our rite!*

Stand tall, with your arms upraised, the blade in your right hand and the crow feather in the left. Then say:

> *Great Morrigan,*
> *I invoke you by your names!*
>
> *Nemhain! Nemhain! Nemhain!*
> *Savage maiden of battle frenzy,*
> *Wild with lust to win;*
> *More beautiful than words can say,*
> *More terrible than death!*
> *You delight in the defeat of armies*
> *And the devastation of the enemy;*
> *You enflame the heroes*
> *To the conquest of evil!*
> *There is poetry in your madness*

And joy in your fighting!
Join with me, lady white as bone,
And sow the seeds of strength!

Great Morrigan,
I invoke you by your names!
Badb! Badb! Badb!
Storm crow on the wild night wind,
Black feathers torn from the heart of darkness!
Rending claws and beak that plucks eyes,
Wings that blind the foe!
Mother of warfare,
Battle goddess,
Whose feast is carrion
From the field of the slain,
Whose joy is victory!
Join with us, lady of scarlet blood,
And reap the harvest of struggle!

Great Morrigan,
I invoke you by your names!
Macha! Macha! Macha!
Great queen of phantoms,
In whose wild train
Follow all the defeated!
Lady of air and darkness,
Whose boon companions
Are the ghosts of the dead!
Banshee howling in the night,
Whose panic fear sets all evil ones to flight
With terror screaming in their throats!
Washer at the ford of rivers
Omen of conquest!
Join us, lady black as death,
And winnow stern seed from the chaff!

Feel the powers you have invoked cover and fill you. You are the fiery goddess of battle; you ride the black horse of power. You stand stern, powerful and invincible! Feel all oppressors and evildoers fall before your lightning and your sword! None can defeat you! Place the feather in your hair, hold your blade with both hands, and become the goddess, saying:

> I am Great Morrigan,
> I am the warrior goddess and
> I will take the oath of power,
> And drink from the cup
> Of strength!
> The warrior power is in me!
> With weapon raised!
> I am one body,
> One blood, one mind,
> Vowed to protect the innocent
> And defeat all my foes!
> By the sacred cauldron of Dagda
> The blood I have shed in my life
> The power I have unleashed
> As Morrigan
> I vow to be strong and to fight
> With honor
> Power
> And honesty!

Pour the last of the wine out upon the ground. Say:

> I am of royal blood,
> I am the great queen of battle!
> I win the fight that must be fought every day,
> And the wedding won every night!
> I am victorious and empowered
> The one who survives all battles!
> Now, and always!
> So may it be!

Sit and meditate on this power that is now yours. Plunge your blade into the earth and let the energy pass from you, knowing that it will always be with you and can be called forth at any time! When you have come down and the power has left you, take up your blade again and say:

> As a warrior Priestess of Morrigan
> I go forth to ward the ways
> To stride confident and powerful
> Into my life and the world.
> I shall win mighty victories
> I shall never truly be defeated
> I shall work wonders in the world!
> Thanks to Morrigan
> To her aspects Macha! Badb! Nemhain!
> May I be strong
> Yet compassionate
> Fierce
> Yet merciful
> Powerful
> Yet joyful!
> So mote it be!

Blow out the candle and the incense. Using the spade, bury everything but the feather. Leave this stuck in the ground in that place. Go forth and be a warrior!

THE GODDESS
Oshun

ORIGIN: Yoruba (African)
ATTRIBUTES: feminine beauty and kindness
COLOR: gold and red
SYMBOL: a small hand mirror
ELEMENT: water
STONE/METAL: amber and red coral
SCENT: orange or chamomile

INTRODUCTION

That first impression is so important, no matter whom you are going to meet. Call upon the goddess Oshun if you desire to look so memorable that no one can stop admiring your great beauty. In fact, all eyes will be upon you when you glide into a crowed room with Oshun's power.

Oshun is the Yoruba (African) goddess of beauty and love. She provides you with an inner and outer glow when you must have some well-deserved admiration or attention. Call her when you need your royal subjects to love and worship the ground you walk on. Oshun has a magical quality of beauty in all that she says and does. Oshun is the one to invoke to be beautiful and to have beauty surround you.

The Yoruba goddess of love and beauty is one of the eight goddesses or gods (Orishas) that were sent by Olodumare (god) to watch over the world and its people. Oshun is an important goddess in many different African and Caribbean religions such as Voudoun, Candoble, Santeria, and Shango.

It is said the goddess Oshun lives in rivers and waterfalls, or in any sweet waters. Oshun takes the form of a beautiful, slender African woman who is dressed in yellow, gold, and red. She is graceful, kind, and loving as well as enticing and flirtatious. She always holds a hand mirror and wears strings of yellow and red beads around her neck.

There are many stories about Oshun, but this is one of the best. Laro, an explorer and warrior, was sent west with his people to start a rival outpost along the trade route. When they reached the river crossing called Ofatado ("where the bow and arrow rest"), Laro said to his followers, "Let us put aside our weapons of war and death. Here where we will always find fresh water, let us found a town of our own and forget the harassment of our former existence."

One of Laro's daughters disappeared beneath the water while bathing. Laro, fearing that his daughter was lost forever, stood grieving on a large rock. She reappeared, dressed in a silk saffron gown, with her arms covered with brass bangles. Laro was overjoyed at his daughter's reappearance. Suddenly a large fish leaped into his hand and said, "If you promise not to build here upon my mistress Oshun's sacred bank, but further up on the shores of the river, she will protect your town forever." The fish continued, "Oshun in turn will make your town prosper." Before the fish jumped back into the water, he told Laro not to forget that cornmeal and honey are Oshun's favorite dishes. Laro moved on with his people and founded a town that he named after her called Oshogbo, or "adult Oshun."

Today once a year in the land of the Yoruba (West Africa) a girl is chosen as the sacred Arugba. In a deep trance she walks alone, along a secluded river trail. The Arugba walks like a peacock strutting, so as not to bruise the path she walks down. Two bitter kola nuts are put in her mouth, so that she can keep all she hears a secret. It is here that she visits the Goddess Oshun where she lives. Only the girl's priest can witness this event. The other villagers wait for her to return to another riverbank and use the secrets of the beautiful goddess to help and bless them.

Anytime you want to honor Oshun, decorate a place with beautiful things, perfumes, yellow silks, and a hand mirror, and ask her to dwell there with your blessings. Often she cannot resist a beautiful place, especially if you wear jewelry—lots and lots of it!

* ★ * ★ *

GODDESS OSHUN INVOCATION

Oshun! O goddess Oshun!
Ashe! Ashe! Ashe!
The beauty you bring
The gold that you wear
Brass around your limbs
Ileke necklace of red and yellow
A yellow silk dress is wrapped
Around you when you strut
Like a peacock!
The rustling and bustling make music to
My ears, O lovely one.
In your hand is a mirror
You stop to admire yourself
And in your other hand is fan of
Peacock feathers.
You fan yourself
I feel it as a cool river mist!
Ashe! Oshun! Bless me!

I call out your name Oshun
To ask that you stay
And bless and dwell
In this place of beauty
Bring out my beauty
Bring beauty to me!
Beautiful goddess
With sweet water
Swirling around your legs
And washing your feet

Cool water
Lovely goddess
Kind to everyone she meets
Be kind to me!
Ashe-O!

Gentle water one
Who holds the secrets
Of eternal beauty
And love
Dance is sacred to you
Decoration and yellow silk
Make you the loveliest
Goddess of the Orisha.

All are charmed by your
Beauty and all want to
Be near your side
No one is turned away.
Oshun is forever
The gentlest of all
The one who loves
Ashe Oshun!
Come by your many names!
The goddess of elegance
Oshun kile kile
The goddess of seduction
Oshun awe
Oshun Orisha!
Great goddess Oshun!
Fill us with love and beauty
Accept our prayers and offerings!
Ashe-O!

GODDESS OSHUN VISUALIZATION EXERCISE

You are in a misty, warm, scented jungle.
The jungle ferns
Surround you as you
Follow the sounds of a peacock
Screaming its cry.
You push back the ferns
From your face.
The sunlight sparkles
As it makes patterns of light
Dance on the river in front of you.
Closer to the rushing
River you come to see where the
Peacock has gone.
The bird flies up into a nearby tree
Its beautiful tail feathers reach
To the ground even though the
Peacock is on the highest branch.
The bird cries again, then it shakes its
Tail feathers at you like a fan.
One tail feather falls to the ground and you pick it up,
Holding it into your hand.
A peacock fan.

The iridescent colors resemble those
Of the river
The peacock winks at you
And you nod your head
And strut like a peacock to
The riverbank,
Where Oshun lives.

The cool sweet water
Surrounds you as you wade in the
River to meet the goddess of beauty.

Standing in the middle
Of the river is Oshun.
Her yellow silk dress
Floats to the top of the water,
Billowing like a cloud.
She looks ethereal in her domain.

She wears brass and gold jewelry.
Coral and amber beads
Adorn her, and a mirror is in her hand.
She takes the mirror and shows you
Your image, and never have you looked
So radiant and beautiful.
Hand her the peacock feather in your hand.
Hand it to the goddess in thanks.
She winks at you and as you smile,
You tell her your secrets, everything
Oshun is known never to tell
A soul,
And in return she gives you beauty
And allure!
It is time to say good-bye for now.
You part company and leave.
Oshun stays in the river
And you walk to the riverbank,
Following the cries of the peacock,
And into the jungle you go.
Ferns surround you as you sway
Back into the forest,
Back into your room,
Still tingling with
Beauty!

Oshun Goddess Empowerment Ritual: Becoming Beauty and Glowing Loveliness

Oshun is always lovely and she is the personification of beauty, charm, and love. If you have any misgivings about how lovely you really are, then call on the powers of this very powerful, kind deity. The Oshun empowerment will make you feel beautiful inside and out, no matter what your imperfections may be. This is the first step in eradicating body shyness.

You Will Need

- ◉ a yellow cloth
- ◉ an image of Oshun
- ◉ a gold and red beaded necklace
- ◉ yellow roses
- ◉ perfumes
- ◉ cosmetics
- ◉ soap
- ◉ a towel
- ◉ a small amount of honey
- ◉ chamomile tea (a tea bag)
- ◉ a hand mirror
- ◉ cornmeal
- ◉ jewelry
- ◉ matches
- ◉ yellow candle
- ◉ beautiful clothes to put on
- ◉ an offering of oranges and honey

The Ritual

The place where you call to her must be clean and beautiful. Lay down the yellow cloth first, then her image, the beads, and also provide a rose or two. Make it beautiful! Use any special luxury item that you love, things like perfume that help you feel more beautiful, as your ritualistic tools. The best place to set up Oshun's altar is in front of a vanity or in a bathroom. Be ready to take a special magickal bath and put on makeup.

Oshun is here to beautify you and to silence the inner critic once and for all.

Pick out with care what you are going to wear on the day or night of your debut as beauty queen. Cosmetics, soap, bath towels—everything should be fancy and pleasing to look at.

Fill up the bathroom sink with water and add a little honey and a bag of chamomolie tea to sweeten the water. As you splash the water on your face, say:

> *Ashe Ashe Ashe!*
> *I call the Goddess Oshun*
> *Beauty is your domain*
> *No one is lovelier than you*
> *Make me beautiful in all ways*
> *O goddess of sweet waters*
> *Orisha of beauty!*
> *Come and bless me*
> *Accept my offerings*
> *Come in beauty, Oshun*
> *Ashe-O!*

Sprinkle a little of the water to the four directions and around the altar. Then dry off your face and look in the mirror. Apply a touch of cornmeal to your face and again repeat the same verse above. Sprinkle a little cornmeal over your altar. Put the red and gold beaded necklace on.

Then, apply all your makeup and put on your jewelry. Pose naked as a goddess, saying:

> *Ashe Ashe Ashe!*
> *I am the Goddess Oshun*
> *Beauty is my domain*
> *No one is lovelier than me*
> *I am beautiful in all ways*
> *I am the goddess of sweet waters*
> *I am Orisha of beauty!*
> *I am blessed!*
> *I walk in beauty as Oshun*
> *Ashe-O!*

Now light a yellow candle and pick up the hand mirror. While you look in the mirror, say:

I am the great Goddess Oshun
I live in fresh water
Rivers, lakes, and streams
I am a beautiful woman
Others desire me as their queen.
I am gentle and kind to many
Who ask favors of me
Always a charming lady
I never act aggressively.
Others notice my presence
When I strut into a room,
All eyes are upon me
Men and woman whisper
Among themselves when I appear
Who is that lovely goddess? they say.

I am gorgeous
Exciting, inciting am I,
I love all things of beauty
I grace all lovely things
Yeye onikii, obalodo
I am the queen of the river
I am the royal one
The beauty goddess
of yellow and gold.

Palms are my plant
The peacock is my bird
A fan of duck feathers.
And most important
Of all is what
I treasure, my hand mirror.
I am Oshun
The beauty queen of them all
Tell me all your secrets

And your hidden gloom
Whisper your desires
And I will relieve your
Sadness with love, for
Beauty is my balm.
I will give love freely
As long as you adorn
Finery and decor.
I love pretty dresses,
Jewelry, and cosmetics.
I am Oshun
I love creativity in dress and self-adornment
I am transformed to beauty
I am pretty when I am appreciated
Loved and adored
I love to be honored in decorating
My home and temple
I will bless any beautiful space
I am Oshun and I reign!
Ashe-O!

Now and wave the mirror like a magickal wand over your beautiful clothes, and say:

I am Oshun and I bring power as:
Yeye kari.
Mother of the mirror,
Yeye 'jo . . .
Mother of dance,
Yeye opo.
Mother of abundance
Bless this sacred raiment
That beauty may walk the land!

Put the mirror down and put your beautiful clothes on. After you are dressed in loveliness, say:

> *Ashe!*
> *I am beauty I am Oshun*
> *The goddess of beauty*
> *Inside as well, true beauty*
> *Reigns inside of me I have*
> *An inner glow that I feel*
> *Like a young bride and*
> *My inner beauty glows*
> *That I dazzle strangers*
> *And friends alike.*
> *Everyone is captivated*
> *I am Oshun*
> *A gorgeous lady am I*
> *Others watch me as I*
> *Smile so graciously*
> *I am the queen of beauty and*
> *Nobody forgets me!*
> *Ashe!*

Holding the mirror high, turn slowly clockwise, shining as the sun in your beauty! You are Oshun and you delight the world! Slowly return back to being "you" and as you do so, lower the mirror and leave it face-down. Sprinkle a little water over it. Bow before the image of the goddess and make an offering to her of oranges and honey. Thank her for this loveliness! Say:

> *Ashe Ashe Ashe!*
> *Praise to you great Orisha of Beauty!*
> *O goddess Oshun*
> *Beauty is your domain*
> *No one is lovelier than you*
> *You are beautiful in all ways*
> *Thank you for this blessing!*
> *Accept my prayers!*

May I always walk in beauty
As a peacock
A golden jewel
A mirror of lovliness!
Ashe-O!

Blow out the candles, and let the water go down the sink. Put away your things of beauty and go out and charm the world!

THE GODDESS Pele

* *

ORIGIN: Hawaiian
ATTRIBUTE: intensity in love and life
COLOR: orange/red
SYMBOL: volcano
ELEMENT: fire
STONE/METAL: obsidian
SCENT: hibiscus, ylang ylang, or mango

* *

INTRODUCTION

Pele is the Hawaiian volcano goddess, and she is one active hot lady. Need to stir up some romantic heat in you life? Want to take a walk on the wild side? Maybe you are tired of always being a good girl? Then take off your reading glasses, shake your mane free, kick off your sensible shoes, go barefoot, and get lei-ed! If you desire a wild, impetuous, and passionate nature, then Madame Pele may be for you.

Pele is a wild and passionate goddess who is worshipped even today by thousands in Hawaii. When the people of Hawaii honor her, they throw hibiscus leis (garlands), sugarcane, and gin into her crater. You can also give her other offerings of choice as long as they are wrapped in tea leaves. Pele demands respect on her scared grounds. She lives on the Big

Island at Hawaii Volcanoes National Park. Yes, you can visit her, but do not take from her sacred land! Each year thousands of visitors come to see her and some take stones from her. Many of the items are returned with a note sent to "Madam Pele." The post office on the Big Island receives packages almost every day from around the world full of volcanic rocks or black sand taken from her home, the national park. Bad luck happens to those who take something from her and do not ask. The thieves are only more than relieved to dump what has caused them misfortune, and ask for her forgiveness.

Pele's other names are *Pele-honua-mea,* "Pele of the sacred land," and *Pele-'ai-honua,* "Pele the eater of land." Madame Pele, or TuTu Pele (TuTu is a affectionate name for grandmother), is also known by her spirit name, *Ka-'ula-o-ke-ahi,* or "the redness of the fire."

Pele is originally from Polynesia and came to the island of Hawaii when her earth goddess mother, Haumea, sent her away. She was worried that Pele would be threatened by her sister Namaka, the ocean goddess. Pele seduced Namaka's husband, and her sister was furious with her. Pele, a fire-loving erotic girl, caused problems at home when she played with fire in the underworld. Pele's sister Namaka was furious about the destruction of their home.

Haumea sent Pele out in a canoe led by her shark god brother Kamoho-ali to escape her sister. Pele needed a place to live, so she took out her divining rod of fire and stuck it into the ocean, which caused eruptions from under the sea. The volcano rose up, erupted, and then formed the Hawaiian Islands. Each time Pele put her fire rod in the ground, her sister Namaka found her. Pele was eventually defeated by her sister. Her sprit rose from her body and her soul flew into the crater of Kilauea, or Halemaumau Volcano.

Pele always had a tempestuous sex life. She was courted by and finally married to the Forest God Kamapua'a, who was also her sworn enemy! It has been said that they were complete opposites of each other, he being a god of rain, moisture, and living things. Kamapua'a was known as a huge boar with eight eyes, a good-looking man, or the fish called Humuhumu-nukunuku-'a-pua'a, which had thick scales to protect it from lava poured into the sea. Besides being a volcanic goddess, Pele is also the patroness of the hula, the sacred ritual dance used to honor all the gods.

There are many songs and dances about Pele's life. Ohelo berries, which grow around and near her, are sacred to her. Sightings of Pele as a red-robed woman dancing the hula on the crater rims, or as an old woman, sometimes with a white dog beside her, are still common. We call on Pele to enflame lust, to add sparks to a smoldering romance, to incite wild love and exciting amorous adventures. Honor her and be honest and all will be fine, but don't diss her! She is a proud and fiery goddess!

* ★ * ★ *

$\mathcal{I}$NVOCATION TO THE GODDESS PELE

TuTu Pele!
Ola Pele!
Haiiaka Pele!
Heed my prayer!
Fiery one erupting from the sea
Primal energy and passion
Flow like lava and roll into the sea.
Tahiti is your birthplace
Across the ocean you come
In a canoe with your siblings
Ka-moho-ali your brother
The shark god leads the way.
Quickly you paddle
Your sister Namaka the ocean
Goddess pursues you
Extinguishing your every flame.
In your arms you carry your beloved
Baby sister, Hi'iaka, inside an egg.
When she emerges from her shell
The sprit of dance is she.
TuTu Pele
Patroness of the hula and songs
And dances have been created for you
Lovely, flirtatious, fire goddess
Are you.

I call out to you
Madame Pele and I offer you
Ohelo berries in spirit.
Above you soars a hawk
Near your side is a white dog
TuTu Pele!
I honor you!
Some have picked you up at the roadside
Then you rode in the back of their car,
Then you were gone
Goddess of the volcanoes
Seducer of common men
Lover of many
You fight for what is yours
Madame Pele.
TuTu Pele
The creator of land
Your red-hot lava boils over
And pours out over your blackened sand
As passions flow
Inside of me!
May you be pleased!
May I honor you!
Ae Akua!
Ae Akua!
Ae Akua!

* * * * *

GODDESS PELE VISUALIZATION EXERCISE

You approach an island in a tropical sea.
There is a volcano erupting gently on it.
In the fiery crater sits a goddess
Laughing and dancing.
You come near and whisper to her:
"Pele, I see you

With your black
Lava hair and
Shiny coils reaching out to the sea,
Steaming.
Pele, you make the land for your people
Spirit that you are,
Still active, spilling your
Fire into the atmosphere,
Rubbing underneath and preparing
To make larger your volcano!
Hail to you, O Pele!"
You see now it is a beautiful emerald island
Surrounded by the azure sea.
The sky holds Pele's fire
Like a ruby cast into the sun.
Her heat radiates and warms
Like an egg of creation.
You can see, feel, and taste
Your own heat and passion
Rising around you.
Pele reaches out, smiling.
See her passion reflected in you.
She places a crown of hibiscus flowers
On your head,
A lei of sweet-smelling flowers
Is roped around your neck,
Sour ohai berries she feeds you.
You are surrounded by ferns and palm trees
Swaying in the breeze.
You are one with
The tropical paradise of Hawaii.
You can smell Pele's sulfur.
Feel the heat of her hot air.
Sparks fly,
Cinders circle in the air.
You rise and keep a safe distance.

Fascinated, you want to come near,
But the volcano is erupting,
Flames and lava flying.
As you rise you see Pele emerge
From this fiery chaos as a young woman,
Dancing the sacred hula in a grass skirt,
Exotic flowers on her breast,
Dancing on the rim.
The red glow surrounds both of you as a halo.
Pele's spirit is alive.
Your spirit is enflamed with passion!
From mists and smoke you return,
Vibrating with fiery energy
Of lust and joy!

★ ★ ★ ★ ★

Goddess Pele Empowerment Ritual: Becoming Passion and a Power of Respect

If you want to feel lustful, and still get respect, then Pele is the goddess for you. While I am writing this chapter, not only did I ask for permission to cosmically interview her, but I also am wearing a lei of orchids and tuberoses. I honor her to become one with Queen Pele and get into the aloha spirit. I feel her now! So will you.

When you get to become the goddess Pele, you can finally put those tiki glasses to good use and make yourself a gin drink. (She loves gin!) Put on some Hawaiian dancing clothes because you are going to need them with this goddess. Don't forget that you should wear red. Also do not forget to wear flowers, too. Leis are the best!

You Will Need
◉ volcanic rock
◉ a walking stick (bamboo is great)
◉ matches
◉ a red candle

- hibiscus or rose incense
- gin or ginger ale
- hibiscus and other tropical flowers to wear
- bananas
- an image of Pele

The Ritual

Do this ritual outside if all possible, especially in a place that has volcanic rock if you can. If you must do this inside, have a piece of volcanic rock on your altar, which should face in the direction of Hawaii. Assemble all your items in a pleasing way, wear red, and relax. Meditate on the image of Pele.

To begin the ritual, take the stick and hit the ground five times, saying each time you hit the ground:

> *Aloha Pele—I call Pele-honua-mea, Pele of the sacred land!*
> *I call Pele-'ai-honua, Pele the eater of land!*
> *I call Madame Pele!*
> *I call TuTu Pele, Pele the grandmother!*
> *I call Ka-'ula-o-ke-ahi, Pele the redness of the fire!*

Now light the red candle and incense, saying:

> *Pele arise and fill this heiau!*
> *Your passionate feelings*
> *Erupt and spill over*
> *Extinguishing all that is in your way.*
> *Your sulfur and steam surround me and I draw on the energy*
> *It is from your fiery emotions that I gain my strength.*
> *Now you have found the hidden strength*
> *Deep below where the crater lives*
> *You will fight for what is yours*
> *You are volatile when bothered*
> *You also create such loveliness!*
> *I look at the beauty*
> *Of the land you create*
> *Tutu Pele! O passionate lover*
> *O jealous rival*

> *And queen and creator of the land*
> *Pelle Kakui!*
> *Accept these offerings!*
> *Be here now to empower me*
> *With your passion and power!*

Sprinkle a bit of gin over the offerings of flowers, walking stick, and volcanic rock. Now get ready to dance a simple hula of your design. Use your whole body and become the goddess! Say:

> *Ae Aku!*
> *I am Pele!*
> *I am Pele-honua-mea, Pele of the sacred land*
> *I am Pele-'ai-honua, Pele the eater of land*
> *I am TuTu Pele, Madame Pele or TuTu Pele,*
> *I am Ka-'ula-o-ke-ahi, the redness of the fire*
> *I the Goddess Pele make*
> *Beauty, and*
> *I create all land and passion*
> *I ask for respect*
> *And demand it!*
> *Woe to the one*
> *Who does not respect me!*
> *Ae Akua!*
> *I see myself as one who needs to be respected*
> *Never have I been jilted or scorned*
> *Respect me like the goddess I am*
> *Do not snub or ignore me*
> *I am Madame Pele*
> *Listen to eruption!*

Keep dancing, saying:

> *I demand my right to be*
> *Treated as an equal*
> *That others ask my permission*
> *For my blessings!*
> *I feel the heat deep inside me*
> *Where my warmth is the strongest*

The passion that has lain deep within me
That has been dormant for too long
I am a red-hot mama
Spewing forth molten ashes and lava from the ground
I am love and erotic power!
Waiting to be awoken and
Released into the atmosphere
I am a fireball
I am Pele!
The lovely beauty who is
Dangerous and lethal
To the disrespecting
I give them bad luck
Wherever they may fall
I am Pele
TuTu Pele
Fire! Love! Respect! Passion
Ae Akua!

Fall to the ground before the altar and smolder there! Your dance is done. Offer it to Pele as you become "you" and return to normal consciousness. Meditate on the experience. When you have finished, rise and say:

Thank you, Pele!
Your power resides as a flame
A red flower
A sacred berry
A volcano
A smile of lust
Glowing in my heart forever!
Ae O TuTu Pele!

Now, take the stick again, and each time hit the ground as you say her name.

Aloha Pele—I call Pele-honua-mea, Pele of the sacred land!
I call Pele-'ai-honua, Pele the eater of land!
I call Madame Pele!

I call TuTu Pele, Pele the grandmother!
I call Ka-'ula-o-ke-ahi, Pele the redness of the fire!

Now blow out the candle and incense, and leave the stick stuck in the earth. Leave the flowers, eat the bananas, and drink up the gin. Go and be passionate and respected!

THE GODDESS
Persephone

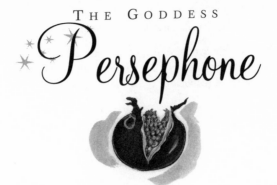

* * * * * * * * * * * * * * * * * * *

ORIGIN: Greek
ATTRIBUTE: overcoming obstacles
COLOR: deep purple
SYMBOL: pomegranate
ELEMENT: air
STONE/METAL: clear quartz crystal
SCENT: pomegranate or hyacinth

* * * * * * * * * * * * * * * * * * *

INTRODUCTION

Life brings us trials and sadness, losses of people and dreams as well as challenges we must rise to meet and overcome. In dealing with losses and with life challenges, we must cultivate an acceptance of the struggles of life and the ability to let go of loss and pain, and transcend them. If you need to cultivate these attitudes, call upon Persephone, for she literally lost the world but triumphed to become a symbol of transcendence! Goddess of transformations and long journeys (both spiritual and earthly), she has literally been to Hades and back and returns with the power to bless you with the power of transcendence and overcoming.

In the late Homeric form of Greek mythology, Persephone is the daughter of Demeter and Zeus. She is the power of new life in the spring, the hidden mystery of the living spirit underground that returns to life in the new planting after the death of winter. She is also called Kore, the ever-youthful maiden, who dances with her companions through fields of flowers. She is the rejuvenation of the world. Yet she also represents an older and somewhat deeper mystery; she is the queen of the land of the dead and overcoming death.

Of old, the goddess ruled the sky, the earth, and beneath the earth, the three realms of existence. While her form evolved with the coming of later gods, she still retains her ancient powers. It is she who was taken to Hades and returned. In some of the ancient mystery cults it was believed that initiates could make the journey to Hades while still living, and there they would find great wisdom and life renewed. The underworld was the land of the dead, but was it also the womb of rebirth, where souls prepared for reincarnation.

Hades, her consort, is in a sense the infernal reflection of celestial Zeus, and because Hades's subterranean kingdom contains the gold, silver, and jewels of the world, he is often seen as the giver of wealth. As we tire of the old routines in our life, we may call upon the eternal renewer Persephone to help us overcome the deep problems and obstacles we face! Persephone is the giver of renewed life and bravely stood up to Hades and melted his heart with the acceptance of her fate and transcended the limits imposed upon her. In this way she became queen of the underworld for six months a year, but rises every spring to join her mother, Demeter, as the goddess of renewed life, triumphant over death. Her flower is the poppy, her fruit the pomegranate. Both symbolize renewal. Her candles should be dark purple. Call on Persephone when you want to overcome difficulties or banish the blues.

* * * * *

$\mathcal{I}$NVOCATION OF PERSEPHONE

Persephone! Persephone! Persephone!
Kyria Kore hear us!

Guardian of the world unseen,
Queen of mystery and night
Who holds the keys of death and birth

And that which is beyond,
I call you!
Help me to let go
Overcome
And transcend!

You who guard the gates of Hades
And receive as guests
Those who pass beyond;
You who bring compassion
And inner strength
To those burdened with life;
You who bring the cup of memory
And the mercy of forgetfulness,
I call you!
Help me to let go
Overcome
And transcend!

Goddess who wanders in the fields,
Gathering asphodel and narcissus
In the light of the sun;
Bride who rides the dark descent,
In the chariot drawn by black horses
By the light of the waning moon;
Queen enthroned in the underworld,
Who guides souls in silence
Beneath the stars of night,
I call you!
Help me to let go
Overcome
And transcend!

Dark of hair and pale of skin,
Most beautiful goddess
Desired by death;
Robed in white and cloaked in black,
Jeweled with silver serpents

Your eyes are ruby flame;
You are seated upon a throne of white
In the secret place beneath the world,
Beyond the crossing of the river Styx,
I call you, Persephone!
Help me to let go
Overcome
And transcend!

Reveal the mystery
Of the buried seed
Which leaps to life,
Show me the secret
Of eternal rebirth
And childhood's end,
Take me beyond
The turning wheel
To the still point of knowing.
I call you!
Help me to let go
Overcome
And transcend!

Persephone! Persephone! Persephone!
You who triumphed over Hades
And have returned to the light of the living world
Bless me, heal me, help me overcome!
Kyria Kore!

* * * * *

Goddess Persephone Visualization Exercise

You stand in the caverns of the underworld,
The home of dead souls
And the palace of death's rulers.
About you stretches a vast and misty plain
Whose horizon cannot be seen;

A field of passing formless shades
Who wander without destination,
Mourning their past lives lost
And grieving for the sunlit lands.
They are the ghosts of memory and desire,
The broken shards of incarnation.
No sunlight burns here
Nor changing moon,
But only ageless twilight dimly glows.

Among the misty human shapes
You now see other forms as well:
The echoes of your past,
Of all those who have gone before
Down the long corridors of eternity
Which lead to the gate called oblivion.
With ponderous tread the past goes by.
The ghosts of memory,
They go not alone into the night.
Men, women, and children,
All who have passed away,
All who are born shall someday die,
All who know life shall know sorrow of death.

And death is the lady of night and sighs,
Who comes like the wind in the trees, unseen;
Whose pale hand comforts the tortured brow
And cools at last the fevered child;
Invisible walker in every shadow,
Unknown companion and friend
Who brings the mercy of release
Of letting go and accepting the dark,
Thus ending suffering,
Bringing the peace of transcendence.
Pale as the scythe of the waning moon,
Silent and secret and darkly garbed,
She watches and waits

For appointed fates
Offering the poppy of forgetting and of release.

The shadow of her presence
Falls coolly upon you,
Like shadows in midnight rivers.
All petty concerns and fears wash away
And leave you strong as white bone.
When a warrior of life
Makes death a companion
There is no more time to waste,
And all decisions are final.
You must do only what you should do
To give love and compassion and make art.

You gaze upon darkness
And the travails of earth,
Dry trees and skeletal bones.
Yet out of the mercy of the unseen queen
Change comes over the changeless realm
And souls return to life.
Soft notes of the pan pipes
Call over the ruins.
The soft green light grows
Brighter and stronger.
The dying earth is reborn.
As the light increases, the spirits fly.
All over the world dead trees show new leaves
And barren wombs stir with life.
Purged of poison, the earth and sea
Begin again their turning dance,
The sea-birds cry above the shore
And the music of the waves is heard.
The waning moon begins to wax,
And out of death comes life.
New growth arises from decay.
You awaken to a new life,

To the acceptance of things,
To the joy that living brings,
Free of shadows, fears, and regrets!
And again the tide is turning,
And the light grows brighter with dawn,
The brilliant light of day,
Of Kore,
The reborn Persephone!

* * * * *

EMPOWERMENT RITUAL OF THE GODDESS PERSEPHONE: JOURNEY TO THE UNDERWORLD AND BACK—THE POWER OF RENEWAL

This ritual is designed as one of the more initiatory experiences in this book, and it is presented as a drama of the soul's journey to the land of the dead and back. Before we can effectively work on being successful in our lives, we must confront our pain and challenges, let go of them, and transcend them. We can do this by becoming aware of our inner darkness and shadows and accepting them. The underworld is the place inside us where we hide what we need to confront, let go of, accept, and transcend. To enter here and emerge transformed is to evolve. Persephone will help you!

This is a very old story, told in almost every world mythology. Sometimes it is one of the gods who descends, at others the heroine or hero. In either case, the message is the same: Death may be overcome by the one who knows the mysteries, and new life arises from the passing of the old. The earth, which appears to die with the coming of winter, is reborn as the wheel turns to spring, the departed soul returns in a new form, and the darkness of sorrow passes away.

You Will Need
⊚ dark clothing and a veil to wear
⊚ matches
⊚ any dark and earthy incense, like musk
⊚ two coins on the altar

- a purple candle
- chalices of water and wine
- a veiled mirror
- white flowers and pomegranate seeds
- an image of Persephone

The Ritual

Perform this ritual in a dark and hidden place, such as a cavern or cave. A grove of trees by a stream or spring by night would serve as well. In modern times a cellar or curtained room is easier to arrange and will work too. Lay out all the items on a stone or a small mound of earth before the veiled mirror.

Dressed in dark clothing, wearing a sheer dark veil, sit in darkness and do deep meditative breathing while contemplating death as both a personal and a universal phenomenon. Begin the drama by burning the incense and saying:

> *We are surrounded by darkness*
> *Husband and mate of Persephone*
> *I name you Hades,*
> *The ruler of the realms below.*
> *I call on you to grant peace to the weary at the end of the road,*
> *Give wealth of secrets to those who learn your ways.*
> *Let me pass through the dark gateway that you guard*
> *And learn the mystery of the land of death;*
> *Let me walk with the messenger of the gods*
> *And may I return from the silent places.*
> *I know the touch of death!*
> *Heiros heiros heiros!*

Take the coins in your hand, touch them to your eyes, and enter the dark realm. Then say:

> *O ferryman over the Styx,*
> *The river whose waters give death.*
> *Bound and blind, you take the living to face death;*
> *I pay my fee to pass this way.*
> *Heiros heiros heiros!*

Toss the coins over your head into the darkness. Pass across "the waters." Light the candle, saying:

> *It is my will to conquer fear,*
> *To pass beyond death,*
> *To learn the secret of life*
> *To overcome the darkness and be renewed*
> *Heiros heiros heiros!*

Offering flowers and fruit, call upon Persephone:

> *Look upon me now:*
> *O dark face of the goddess,*
> *The maker of endings to balance beginnings,*
> *The dark womb of death before life.*
> *I call you, Kore, called also Persephone,*
> *The seed of new grain,*
> *White lady of winter*
> *Who wakes again with summer.*
> *I call you the true Earthspirit or renewal!*
> *I call you the white bone,*
> *I call you the red blood,*
> *I call you the black night before dawn.*
> *May I enter your kingdom*
> *O guide of my soul!*
> *Kyria Kore!*

Touch the two chalices to each other. Take up the chalice of wine, hold it high, and say:

> *Two cups do you offer me O Persephone!*
> *The first is called lethe,*
> *And it holds the waters*
> *That rise from the well of forgetfulness*
> *That stands by the gate of ivory.*
> *Here is the end of all sorrow and struggle,*
> *The end of the pain of living and dying,*
> *Sweet wine of oblivion.*
> *May drink and forget and release*
> *Troubles and pain have known?*

Pick up the cup of water, saying:

> *It is my will to conquer fear,*
> *To pass beyond death,*
> *To learn the secret of life*
> *To let go and transcend!*
> *Heiros heiros heiros!*

Drink deeply and close your eyes. Feel your pain and troubles pass away. Say:

> *I have passed the second test,*
> *Which is wisdom.*
> *Sorrow makes men deny the world,*
> *Where all must struggle for victory.*
> *Let my soul be loosed,*
> *That I may act as I will!*

Remove your veil, and say:

> *A second cup is offered now:*
> *It is called mnemosyne, and it holds the waters*
> *Which rise from the well of memory*
> *That stands by the gate of horn.*
> *Comfort I will find here,*
> *For in life is struggle and overcoming,*
> *Sweet victory and transcending pain!*
> *I will drink and remember the true joy of life!*

Drink the wine and remember the real meaning and joy of life. Say:

> *It is my will to conquer fear,*
> *To pass beyond death,*
> *To learn the secret of life*
> *To let go and transcend!*
> *Heiros heiros heiros!*

Open your hands and say:

> *Well have I chosen the sacred path*
> *Of the twice-born ones who conquer death.*
> *This is initiation into the sacred mysteries*
> *Of ancient times in many lands;*

This is the passing through change without dying.
I drink deep
And gaze upon the face of my true self
As Persephone!
I am Kore the renewer!
I am Panbios, the goddess of all life from death!
I am Persephone, who triumphs over all!
Kyria!
I am she!
Heiros heiros heiros!
I Persephone!

Pull the veil from the mirror so that you may gaze into the eyes of your own reflection for a time. You are Persephone. You have entered the underworld and become the queen of the Inner Kingdom. Look at the reflection of you as the goddess and accept the vision you receive! Stare deeply into the eyes of the goddess; feel her power emanate from you. You have transcended life and death and are beyond them! Then, after a time, when your reflection again becomes "you" and you are no longer the goddess, say:

I crossed the river Styx
And looked upon the face of my unborn being.
Yesterday and tomorrow are one,
Like the symbol of eternity,
The tail-devouring serpent of the endless round.
When I die, I shall remember Persephone
When I am born once more, I shall remember Persephone
The secrets I have won in this place of darkness
Shall never be lost in the light.
I am the renewed life of Earth
As token of my quest and the freedom I have won,
I taste now the seeds of the pomegranate
Which is Persephone's symbol.
The gates of return are now opened for me,
And my true name shall never be lost.

Sprinkle a little wine and water about you, saying:

> *I honor the ferryman over the Styx,*
> *The river whose waters give death.*
> *Now I return to the sunlit lands;*
> *So I pay my fee to pass this way.*
> *Heiros heiros heiros!*
> *Iao!*
> *The light!*

Spiral up and out of your "cave," laughing at escaping the darkness! Blow out the candle and incense. You are renewed and revitalized, and you have begun the journey of letting go and transcendence! Now you can face any challenge head-on with understanding and confidence.

THE GODDESS

Sekhmet

ORIGIN: Egyptian
ATTRIBUTE: real political and social power
COLOR: crimson
SYMBOL: a sphinx or lioness
ELEMENT: fire
STONE/METAL: bloodstone
SCENT: frankincense

INTRODUCTION

A great goddess of ancient Khem (Egypt), Sekhmet is shown with the body of a beautiful woman and the head of a lioness, crowned with the solar disc and the uraeus serpent. Her name means "the powerful one," and she personifies the fierce and destructive heat of the desert sun. In one aspect she was a goddess of battle and warfare who breathed fire upon the enemies of the pharoah at the Battle of Kadesh; in another, she was a goddess of medicine, perhaps with the old idea that the same force that inflicted plagues could also cure them.

Sekhmet literally means "strong lady," and she is the "enforcer" of the gods, wielding the power of the sun to bless or destroy.

She is sometimes called the daughter of Ra, the sun god, the con sort of the creator Ptah, and her son is called Nefertum. She holds the ankh (a looped cross), the symbol of life, in her hand. According to one legend, she came into being as an aspect of the cow goddess Hathor, sent to slay the enemies of Ra (see the Empowerment Ritual for more details); in her more peaceful moments she was sometimes associated with the cat-headed Love Goddess Bast. As a solar goddess, she is identified with the sun.

One myth that tells much about the power and intensity of this primal lioness goddess is the time she almost destroyed all the people on the Earth. The gods were unhappy with all the chaos that human beings were spreading across creation, especially when they began to plot against the very gods themselves! The God Ra is said to have called together all the gods who felt humans should be punished. Thus Ra called upon the destructive "eye of Ra," or Sekhmet, who attacked humanity and slaughtered many of them, drinking their blood and reveling in her power over them! When the gods said, "Enough!" and tried to stop her, they couldn't, because her power was so strong. The gods had to trick her by spilling buckets of red-dyed beer on the desert near her. With joy she jumped upon it, drank it all, and was thus pacified.

Sekhmet ruled as a powerful and much revered goddess in ancient times. Force, fire, spiritual, and political power could all be manifested by powerful women and the particular fierceness of the sun was seen as feminine and powerful.

We call upon Sekhmet for power, whether it be spiritual, personal, sexual, or political. She has traditionally been associated with all of these kinds of force and energy. While many see a powerful feminine force as something to fear, she who calls upon Sekhmet is transformed into a lioness of strength! Strength and power, when combined with true will and positive goals, are what taking control of your life is all about!

$\mathscr{I}$NVOCATION OF THE GODDESS SEKHMET

Sekhmet! Sekhmet! Sekhmet!

Great queen of Khem,
Mighty lady of flame,
Destroyer of enemies,
Eye of the Sun God Ra!
Hear me, I beseech Thee,
O Intense One!
Goddess of Rekht,
Goddess of Pekhet,
Goddess of Set,
Goddess of Rehesaui,
Goddess of Tchar and Sehert!
Unity, energy, vitality: power!
A Ka Dua Sekhmet!
You take the form
Of a magnificent lioness,
Stalking your prey
In the heat of the noontime!
Unity, energy, vitality: power!
A Ka Dua Sekhmet!
You are the avenging
Eye of the sun,
You are the mighty serpent
Who slays the followers of Set!
Unity, energy, vitality: power!
A Ka Dua Sekhmet!
Daughter of Ra,
Beloved of Ptah,
Mother of Nefertum,
I call you!
Unity, energy, vitality: power!
A Ka Dua Sekhmet!
Forceful one

Who is garbed in red,
Who drinks the blood
Of the enemies of the land!
Unity, energy, vitality: power!
A Ka Dua Sekhmet!
Slayer of evil,
Strength of the goddess,
Terrible form of Hathor,
I call you!
Unity, energy, vitality: power!
A Ka Dua Sekhmet!
Mighty in struggle,
You breathe fire on the foe!
The wicked are put to flight
You triumph over all
When you come as uraeus serpent!
Unity, energy, vitality: power!
A Ka Dua Sekhmet!
You who threaten mankind
With the anger of the gods,
Who drive the evil ones
Into the outer desert
Unity, energy, vitality: power!
A Ka Dua Sekhmet!
You who are the eye
Of the Vengeance of Ra,
The lioness who guards
The kingdom of the two lands;
Unity, energy, vitality: power!
A Ka Dua Sekhmet!
I ask for your mercy
On the people,
I ask for your spells
To make me powerful!
Unity, energy, vitality: power!
A Ka Dua Sekhmet!

I offer sweet-smelling
Flowers to you,
Libations of beer
And burning incense!
Unity, energy, vitality: power!
A Ka Dua Sekhmet!
Turn away the wrath of Ra,
That mankind be not destroyed!
Come as Bast, lady of love,
And be gentle and kind to us!
Unity, energy, vitality: power!
A Ka Dua Sekhmet!
Powerful queen,
Mistress of flame,
Lady of heaven,
I call you!
Unity, energy, vitality: power!
A Ka Dua Sekhmet!
Sekhmet! Sekhmet! Sekhmet!

★ ★ ★ ★ ★

Goddess Sekhmet Visualization Exercise

The earth reels
Before the fire of the sun.
Overwhelming heat
Pours from the heart
Of the solar system,
Scorching Mercury,
Turning Venus to a steaming cauldron.
Only on our world
Can life survive;
Our swift rotation
Allows night to cool us
With her silver hand.
The waves of tides

And the thin aura
Of our atmosphere
Save us from perishing
As the moth does
In the candle.
Look upon the sun:
At her heart
A goddess sits
Upon a throne.
She has the body of a woman
And the head of a lion.
She is robed in garments
Red as blood.
She is crowned
With the golden disc
And the great serpent called uraeus,
Which strikes at evil,
The symbol
Of the royal house.
She holds the ankh of life
And the scepter of power.
She looks with fierce joy
At those who seek to do right;
She looks with mercy
And offers the gift of power
To the children of the mother.
She is called Sekhmet,
The powerful one,
Who is the vengeance
Of the gods
And also the mercy of the gods!
Who is pestilence upon the two lands
And the goddess who makes right,
Who teaches the spells
That hold the medicine of healing.
Invoke her for protection

From the monsters of the night journey,
Invoke her as the heart of the sun,
The source of all personal and political power!
She offers power,
Control,
And inner as well as outer strength
To those who dare to embrace her
With joy and confidence!
Now you embrace her light.
You are filled with power! Joy! Confidence!
As you return, hold this power to you.
Take it as your own
And stride forth
To do your will!

* * * * *

$\mathcal{E}$MPOWERMENT RITUAL OF THE GODDESS SEKHMET: BECOMING THE POWER OF THE SUN

To call upon Sekhmet and become her is a work of extreme power and intensity, not to be done lightly or with little thought. Remember that taking power for yourself means you may get more responsibility as well. If you want political power, at work or in the government, be prepared to help others and do the right thing. This is what Sekhmet demands in exchange for her power! If you wish personal power or power in relationships, use that power wisely and under love. Again, this is something Sekhmet demands. To call her and bring her power into yourself is a wonderful, positive, and revitalizing experience for those with the love and the will to own their own power and strive to better their own lives and of those around them. Go for it! Sekhmet rules!

You Will Need
◎ red and gold clothing to wear
◎ a plate of gold or gold color
◎ an image of Sekhmet
◎ a metallic rattle or small tambourine as a rod or staff of power

◉ matches

◉ a red candle

◉ musk incense

◉ reddish beer or orange juice in a golden cup

◉ a red necklace of some kind

◉ red flowers

The Ritual

This ritual reenacts the ancient myth of Sekhmet's origin, and should be read beneath the noonday sun. Wear red and gold clothing to perform the ritual. It can be done in a sun-filled room or, better yet, outside in a dry and warm place. Assemble all the items upon the gold plate, facing south. When ready, meditate on the sun and the power it represents. Without it, no life could exist. Feel that power. Stand and shake the rattle to the four directions, saying:

Khesef Khet Hem Hat Met! Nefer Sekhmet!
Begone all evil and monsters by the power of Sekhmet!

Stand, raise your hands to shoulder level, and say:

At the dawn of time the creator Atum,
Who is both male and female,
Made the world in its wonder
And humankind to live in it.
In the beginning all was well;
Then evil men began to worship
The dark god Set the destroyer,
And to defile and pollute the Earth
And spread injustice and wrongdoing!
The bright God Ra saw this
And great was his anger
He invoked the power of the sun!

Light the candle and incense. Take up the item you're using for a staff or rod of power. With gestures, reenact this story:

He called you forth O Goddess Sekhmet,
Whose body is the heavens.
You came upon the earth in wrath,

You are the eye of Ra,
The eye of the sun,
The eye of power and making right.
You project the uraeus serpent,
You are crown of kings,
Who spits out flame and lightning,
Who brings terror
Upon the wicked.
You are the lady of power!
The powerful one
Who is garbed in red;
The lioness of gold,
The intensity of the sun!
You hunted down the defilers of temples
And the despoilers of cities,
You drove out the offenders
Against the way of peace and truth!
The hunters for sport,
You overcame them as a pestilence
As a crowned serpent
You crushed evil in her coils;
As a great lion
You tore them with your claws
And devoured them
Great was your wrath, O goddess,
Against those who had offended
Against the way of heaven and earth
And the justice of the gods!

Take up the cup and drink some of the beer, saying:
O Sekhmet!
You became drunk on blood
And the frenzy of slaughter,
Wild with the urge to slay!
The people cried out for mercy
And the gods heard:
The God Ra saw your power

And my works;
Great mother of power,
Fill me, empower me,
Bend over me
Carry our words on the winds
That I may do my will with love!
Remember me, as I call your name!
A ka dua
Sekhmet!

Put out the candle and incense. Leave the flowers as an offering. Take up everything else and stride forth with renewed power and purpose, holding the staff. Go forth and work your will!

THE GODDESS
Shakti

ORIGIN: Hindu
ATTRIBUTE: new beginnings and new energy
COLOR: scarlet
SYMBOL: a rising serpent
ELEMENT: fire
STONE/METAL: ruby
SCENT: sandalwood

INTRODUCTION

Need a cosmic energy boost? Feeling stuck or that you're in a rut and need a goddess push to move on or out? Call upon the very power of the universe herself, the Hindu Goddess Shakti!

Shakti is the energy that forms the basis of the universe in Hindu cosmology. Her other common name is Devi, which simply means "goddess." If there is a universal term for the great mother goddess rooted in ancient India, it is this. Shakti or Devi is a goddess whose origin is prehistoric; there is no doubt that these are some of the oldest forms of the goddess ever worshipped.

The term *Shakti* literally means "energy" in the sense that she is the form of all energy and all matter. She is the personified form of cosmic energy from which the universe was formed and by which it still is made and destroyed every second of every day. It is the energy of life, death, and beyond all else, change. Shakti is identified with all aspects of the goddess in Tantrika and Hinduism. She is the goddess unveiled, the pure expression of power and life. It is therefore fitting that her most appropriate form is in every woman. Call upon her when needing to tap that cosmic energy, start something new, or to simply *do* it!

The classical Tantrik creation mythos that embodies these primal forces states that reality, the supreme Om, divides into Shiva and Shakti in the universe. In the human race, they are so deeply joined that they are beyond time and space in a state of nirvana. They separate, and the feminine force or objective reality is perceived as distinct from the subjective reality or the masculine force. Shakti then dances the web of existence-reality, generating from her womb all existing things. The illusion of time and space is then manifested to the subjective: Shiva. And so began the existence of all problems and pleasures; in fact, this was the origin of all of the material world.

It can be seen by this myth that Shakti or Devi is thus the key to all illumination, perception, and liberation. By seeing all of the world around us as the work of the dance of the goddess, we can understand and tap into the primal source. The lesson of Shakti is that all is divine energy. All things change all the time, and no situation or problem is as hopeless as it seems because at any moment all of reality can manifest in any number of different ways.

The kundalini, the bioelectric force symbolized as a snake of fire erupting through the human body in classical texts, is in reality Shakti. This snake is actually the human nervous system activated. By calling forth Shakti, we can effect change in the abstract and in the physical forms. By realizing basic life patterns and the various systems and patterns that manifest energy in our world, we can realize that the Earth and all things are the same: energy. In this way we come to deeper understandings of nature and of ourselves as energy-entwined forces. Thus we can, with the help of Shakti, face and come to terms with what we need to do and be—with power. Call on Shakti to start anything new, and to be up and energized.

INVOCATION OF THE GODDESS SHAKTI

Great goddess of all things
Shakti Ma!
We honor you, love you, and call you.

You are called all things by all people
Millions of names and forms
Countless aspects and elements
Shakti Devi, goddess
We honor you, love you, and call you.

You who are every being
In the forms of energy and matter
We honor you, love you, and call you.

You who are the force that pervades the universe
The fire of atoms and quarks
Wave, particle, and chaos
We honor you, love you, and call you.

Mother of all things
In the form of every mother
In the form of every woman
In the form of the universe
We honor you, love you, and call you.

Life will toward life and energy of life
We honor you, love you, and call you.

Being and not-being
Existence and abyss
Memory, experience, and all forgetfulness
We honor you, love you, and call you.

Core of everything
Genesis of every thought
Essence of all and nothing
We honor you, love you, and call you

Shakti who is moon and sun
The light of all things and star beyond
Who is in fact the very Earth
We honor you, love you, and call you
Bring us the power! Bring us the energy!

You who take
You who give
You who are
You who are not
You who are joy and all pleasure
You who are all pain and ordeals
You who are beyond all that is conceivable
Shakti
We honor you, love you, and call you.

Devi who exists as peace in all beings
We honor you, love you, and call you

Devi who exists as feeling in all beings
We honor you, love you, and call you.

Devi who exists as mind in all beings
We honor you, love you, and call you.

Devi, goddess, Shakti, mother
You who encompass all possibilities
Who are the form of all gods and goddesses
Who in fact is the universe
Source of all
We honor you, love you, and call you
Bring us the power! Bring us the energy!
Great mother
Wherever you are called
Maha Devi
However you manifest
Shakti om!
We honor you, love you, and call you.
Bring us the power!

Bring us the energy!
Shakti namaste!

* * * * *

$\mathcal{G}$ODDESS SHAKTI VISUALIZATION EXERCISE

You are in a black void.
Nothingness surrounds you.
Suddenly there is an unfolding,
A great silent explosion of energy and light.
It fills all of the void with sparkles,
Light and power and energy.
It is the big bang,
It is the creation of the cosmos,
And as it reaches the limits of reality
It begins to spiral,
Slowly at first,
Like a giant galaxy of light,
Vibrating with many colors now,
Glowing with all energies,
All forces,
All powers.
It begins to spin faster
Until it is like a tornado,
A hurricane,
A spiraling, whirling maelstrom of power.
Faster and faster it spins,
Lightning flashing through the body.
Waves and particles fly.
Beams, rays, and sparks whirl.
And the whole thing begins to contract,
Whirling faster,
Glowing brighter,
Pulsing with light and power.
The form compresses further,
Glowing, spinning, pulsing,

Until it forms the body of a beautiful goddess,
Naked and glowing,
Formed of lightning, fire, and electricity,
Eyes glowing sparks,
Smiling mouth a comet trail.
As her body forms
She is dancing
With joy and power and grace.
Lightning bolts fly
From her glowing yoni.
Waves of light are born
From every pore of her perfect body.
From her womb
Are born glowing forms.
They become galaxies—
Stars, planets, comets, moons—
Until her cosmic birth dance
Has filled all of time and space.
She slows her dance
And looks at you.
She opens her left hand,
And there is the cosmos,
Glowing like a green marble.
And around the Earth
Is whirling a storm of energy,
And this forms into a goddess as well,
And it is also her.
All the universe descends as energy
Through the sky
To your continent,
State, and city.
And there you are,
Surrounded by a whirling storm of energy.
And this energy field is her.
It is Shakti;
You are Shakti.

And so
You create all the universe.
You open your mind
As the universe dances
And you dance,
And you are filled with energy!
There are shadows—dispelled
With the touch of energy,
Light, will, and force
By the power of Shakti,
And you are Shakti.
Feel the energy
You are the energy
The energy is all
And so you may do anything
With love and will
And Shakti!

* * * * *

GODDESS SHAKTI EMPOWERMENT RITUAL: BECOMING THE GODDESS ENERGY

To get things done and have fun, you need *energy*! Shakti is pure energy; to become her is to become power. This ritual is to attune you with the goddess as universal energy and to become filled with her joy. Channel this energy to do whatever you wish to do, such as having an enormous amount of pep and time to undertake your latest project and make it a success. Also, a sacred tool (a crystal charm) will be created that can be used in all future spells.

You Will Need
◉ chalk (if needed)
◉ a flower
◉ a found feather
◉ a cup of pure water
◉ a found stone

- ◉ a beautiful flower
- ◉ matches
- ◉ a red candle
- ◉ a crystal
- ◉ a small spade or trowel

The Ritual

Perform this rite at a crossroads, if possible. If inside, draw a cross on the floor in chalk and perform the rite there. Go to the crossroads at sunset and offer a flower, saying:

> *To cross again*
> *Is not to cross*
> *All things intersect here*
> *Time and space*
> *Past and future*
> *Life and death*
> *Love and will*
> *Shiva and Shakti*
> *Ommmmmmmmmmmmmm*
>
> *To the spirit of this place*
> *Help me and empower my rite*
> *To the gods and goddesses of nature*
> *Help me and empower my rite*
> *To the teachers and the ancestors*
> *Help me and empower my rite*
> *Pujayami namah!*

Lay out the items. Place the crystal in your left hand, and as you do so face the East with the feather and say:

> *I see with the crystal vision*
> *Upon this feather of truth*
> *I conjure here and now*
> *By the power of the winds*
> *Jai Shakti! Svaha!*

Face the West with the water and say:

I see with the crystal vision
Upon these tears of Maya
I conjure here and now
By the power of oceans and lakes
That fills the rivers with power
Jai Shakti! Svaha!

Face the North with the stone and say:

I see with the crystal vision
Upon this flesh of trees
I conjure here and now
By the power all living things
That fills the land with energy
Jai Shakti! Svaha!

Face the South with the flower and say:

I see with the crystal vision
Upon this fires of the sun
I conjure here and now
By the power of energy and power
That fills the bioenergy of Earth with life
Jai Shakti! Svaha!

Light the candle in the center. Hold the crystal carefully over this flame and feel the light filling and becoming you. Focus on center with the crystal, saying:

I see with the crystal vision
The power of the air, water, earth, and fire
Birthed by the will of humanity
As Shakti
I conjure here and now
By the power of winds, waters, mountains, and radiations
Here now I become
The spirit of energy filling this earth
Looking within I see the truth
I am Shakti!

> *Take it into my heart*
> *I am Shakti!*
> *And purify the world with my love energy*
> *I am Shakti!*
> *Om! Shakti Hum! Svaha!*

Bless the crystal with the glowing swirling energies of the cosmos that you have become! Touch it to the four symbols you have present and then into the candle flame. Then, carefully leap over the candle flame several times, saying:

> *I am Shakti*
> *Shakti Shakti!*
> *I am thee*
> *Up up the energy is free*
> *Up up the power in me*
> *Dancing flashing*
> *Let it be!*

As you now slowly spiral out, counterclockwise, toss the feather, flower, water, and stone "out." See yourself filling the universe with your energy; see yourself out in the world doing what you will to do! Sit calmly before the candle and let the energies calm, chanting ommmmm.

When the energy has calmed, bring it inside you. As you become "you," blow out the candle and feel the flame inside you. Now you will always secretly be Shakti! Say:

> *Om Shanti Shiva Shakti*
> *Om Shanti Shiva Shakti*
> *Om Shanti Shiva Shakti*
> *Peace!*

Erase the crossroads and collect all the items and bury them in the earth with the spade. Keep the candle and crystal for future Shakti rites!

THE GODDESS Tara

ORIGIN: Tibetan
ATTRIBUTE: healing and meditation
COLOR: emerald green
SYMBOL: lotus
ELEMENT: water
STONE/METAL: jade
SCENT: lotus, waterlily, or vanilla

INTRODUCTION

Looking for a healing goddess? Tara is the best! Whether you are talking about mental, physical, or spiritual healing, Tara will assist you. She is the ultimate goddess of mercy, help, and healing!

Tara is a supremely important goddess in Tibetan Buddhism. As a part of the Buddhist pantheon, she represents the compassion of the Buddha toward all living things. Yet Tara predates Buddhism, and her ancient lineage is one of the greatest and most revered mother goddesses on the earth. Her name means "star" or, in another translation, "to cross over." Both of these names have tremendous symbolic meaning, but the latter is more relevant to the Buddhist ideal of Tara. In this sense she is called the savioress or protector of all living things. It is said that one in peril has but to utter her name to be saved by the swift and merciful intervention of the goddess.

According to Tantrik lore, she especially helps one avoid the traditional eight dangers as outlined in Buddhist teachings: pride, delusion, anger, envy, wrong views, attachment, avarice, and doubt. She is also said to help those who have karmic difficulties and can help one achieve enlightenment quickly. She is often shown bare-breasted, seated upon a full open lotus. Her right foot reaches down to touch and bless the earth while her right hand symbolizes blessing. She holds blooming lotuses in both hands. The most common manifestation of Tara is green Tara, a beautiful green maiden goddess, seated as previously described, often surrounded by Tantrik saints or other aspects of the goddess with a background of trees, mountains, and living green things. She is often invoked for clarity, wisdom, and especially for healing.

Across most of Asia, Tara reigns supreme as the great loving mother, the ultimate divine feminine healer. As such she is called Maha Tara, "great Tara." As the benevolent goddess of healing, helping, rescuing, and shining forth, Tara is called upon to heal the planet and to heal all beings who are injured or in pain. Today this very popular goddess is called on for healing a loved one or for healing yourself.

May we invoke her with a compassionate spirit, may she flow through us all to heal ourselves and others, and may we mirror her compassion and awaken to the many ways we can help and heal in our everyday lives. Her supreme mantra and invocation is this: *Om tare tuttare ture soha!* ("honor and praise to the great goddess Tara"), pronounced: Om TA-REH TOO-TA-REH TOOR-REH SO-HA.

* * * * *

INVOCATION OF THE GODDESS TARA

Praise to Tara
The great mother and provider of all
Energy supreme
In the boundless universe
Star flashing in the heavens
Eyes of lightning

Lotus-born
Tear of the compassionate cosmos
Help me to heal others
Help me to heal myself.

Face like a million moons
Full and bright
Filled with peace and love
Goddess of mercy
We call upon you
In this our hour of need

Goddess of all that is right and true
Scattering blue lotus petals
Laughing with joy and love
Most giving one
Oh perfect crystal mother
Help us to heal others
Help us to heal ourselves.

All the gods worship you
Great mother of the universe
Songs fill your sky
Demons and evil spirits
Are driven away by your joy
Purify the land
Help me to heal others
Help me to heal myself.

You are the great destroyer
Of fear, of failure
Of oppression and disease
Lift the burden of helplessness
Empower us to see potential.

Radiant and joyful goddess
Dancing across the face
Of this troubled planet

Healing as your lotus feet
Tread the lands about us.

O great protector
You who call upon all the powers
All the gods
All the people of the many worlds
Help me to heal others
Help me to heal myself.
You burn as holy fire
Goddess Tara
Purify us in thy flaming embrace
Joy replaces fear
As our doubts disappear

Blissful goddess
Virtuous, honest, and peaceful
As I become you
The ills of the worlds
Run off me as water drops.

Greatest goddess
Upon whom all the gods and peoples rely
Earthspirit mother
Cover and protect me
You form my armor
Fill me and soothe me
Fill me with calm and a will to act
Help me to heal others
Help me to heal myself
Come great mother of all life!

Here is Tara the red, to the South!
Here is Tara the yellow, to the North!
Here is Tara the black, to the West!
Here is Tara the green, to the East!
And here within me
Is Maha Tara, primal Tara, ultimate Tara

Shining as a star in my heart!
Om tare tuttare ture soha! Tara!
Help me to heal others
Help me to heal myself
Om tare tuttare ture soha!

* ★ * ★ *

$\mathcal{G}$ODDESS TARA VISUALIZATION EXERCISE

A giant endless pool is before you,
Calm, still, clear.
The sky is gray.
Time seems to stretch endlessly,
Calm, peace, emptiness.
Suddenly there is a ripple.
In circles it ripples outward from one point.
Slowly something emerges.
It is a giant bud,
Pink and white.
It rises into the sky and there is a sudden breeze,
Warm and perfumed.
It is the primal lotus,
The first manifestation of creation.
Silently, slowly,
The lotus begins to open.
You feel the sky brighten.
Your heart is filled with increasing joy
As the petals peel back.
There is a figure revealed within the center.
It is a beautiful naked woman,
Seated with legs crossed,
Her skin green, her hair onyx-black.
She is bedecked with gold jewelry,
Ornate chains, pendants, and bracelets,
And on her head is a crown of gold.
She sleeps,

And waves of peaceful healing energy and light
Flow from her body.
The sky completely clears,
And you can see that this pond is surrounded
With the ills of the world.
Silently, call her name
("Tara!").
She begins to sigh and stir.
She slowly opens her eyes,
Deep and green and full of love.
She stares at you and smiles.
Silently, call her
("Tara! Heal me!").
She smiles at you,.
And with great compassion
Looks around her at
Your pain and the ills of the earth.
She raises her left hand
And a lotus bud appears.
It begins to grow,
Opening as it grows up and out,
Blue and white,
Glowing with healing energies.
The lotus fills the sky,
Absorbing all pain.
Tara lowers her right hand to her knee
And a lotus bud appears in her palm.
It begins to grow,
Opening as it grows down and out,
Blue and white,
Glowing with healing energies.
The lotus covers the land,
Absorbing all disease and illness,
And the air is filled
With a powerful perfume,
Wonderful and cleansing and healing.

Breathe this and feel the healing!
Tara lowers her right foot
Until it touches the water,
And a lotus appears where her toe touches.
It begins to grow,
Opening as it grows,
Blue and white,
Glowing with healing energies.
The lotus covers the surface of the waters,
Absorbing all emotional pain.
And Tara smiles again,
And a sweet ringing sound is heard.
And the ills of the world
Are transformed and healed!
Smoking factories become trees.
All physical, emotional, mental, and spiritual ills
Are healed, all becoming green and light.
Silently, thank her
("Tara! May it be so!").
And now take the lotus
She is offering you.
Place it in your heart,
There forever to dwell,
The heart of green Tara
To be used for healing
Yourself and others,
And all beings!

Om Tam Tara!

* ⋆ * ⋆ *

$\mathcal{E}$MPOWERMENT RITUAL OF THE GODDESS TARA: BECOMING THE WORK OF HEALING

When you become Tara, you open your heart to the compassion and healing of the mother. The Goddess Tara is the personification of mercy, compassion and healing benevolence. This empowerment is an excellent healing ritual for all times and places. It can also be effective to clarify, and purify, and center yourself before undertaking a great work.

You Will Need

◉ green clothes and accessories to wear
◉ matches
◉ a green candle
◉ a bell
◉ seven small cups of pure water
◉ green foliage
◉ three sticks of pure and natural vanilla incense

The Ritual

Green is the color of this rite. All clothing and accessories should be green. The rite may be held inside, though it will be more powerful in a wooded area outside.

Feel your pain (or that of the person you wish to heal) and the pain of all who suffer. Light the candle, saying:

> *The pain*
> *The sorrow*
> *The illness*
> *I find solace*
> *In the jewel*
> *In the center of the lotus*
> *Here I am I*
> *The wounds are mine*
> *I give compassion*
> *From my heart*
> *Om mani padme hum!*

Stamp your feet. Throw a "thunderbolt" (your energy) to the four directions, and finally to the center, in your mind's eye. Each time, say:

> *Illness begone!*
> *The healing now begins*
> *Within and without*
> *Phadt! Soha!*

Ring the bell three times and say:
> *To the three jewels*
> *The three eyes*
> *The three wheels*
> *The three powers*
> *Will, knowledge, action*
> *The center is the shining diamond*
> *The heart of bliss*
> *May we all attain*
> *Om tam soha!*

Sit and meditate, facing west. Calm your mind. Meditate and let go of anger. Love all things; become Tara. See yourself as a beautiful naked green goddess seated upon a lotus. As Tara you beam healing green light to all every time you utter *tam*. This love you embody heals all around you with compassion and humor, so say:
> *My eyes are open*
> *I am Tara!*
> *I heal this pain*
> *Tam!*

Touch the earth and say:
> *My eyes are open*
> *I see the illnesses*
> *I am Tara, with my hand*
> *I heal this pain*
> *Tam!*

Touch the cups and the water inside them, saying:
> *My eyes are open*
> *I see the burning energies*
> *I am Tara, with my hand*
> *I heal this pain*
> *Tam!*

Hold the foliage up to the sun, saying:
> *My eyes are open*
> *I see the emotional pain*

> *I am Tara, with my hand*
> *I heal this pain*
> *Tam!*

Light the incense and wave it through the air, saying:

> *My eyes are open*
> *I see the spiritual pain*
> *I am Tara, with my hand*
> *I heal, heal, heal this pain*
> *Tam! Tam! Tam!*

Touch the earth, saying:

> *Om tare tuttare ture soha!*
> *I am Tara*
> *I sit upon a lotus of Healing!*
> Tam!

> *I am Tara Tara Tara*
> *Green goddess*
> *Young and delightful*
> *Filled with life, with hope, with love*
> *Great green mother*
> *Embodiment of life force,*
> *The power of all that grows*
> *I beam healing*
> *Burning away all disease.*
> *The power flowing from my brow*
> *Sweeps away all harmful rays*
> *And radiations.*
> *I am green lady of laughter*
> *May life be renewed*
> *May the poisons of the body*
> *Be burned away*
> *Leaving the shining*
> *Clarity of one mind*
> *Om tare tuttare ture soha!*

Ring the bell three times and stand. Turn and cast the inner Tara light about you. In your mind's eye see it fly out, healing, while you chant:

Om mane padme hum!

In your mind's eye, see the world healed of all illness, see whomever you wished to heal healed of illness, and see yourself healed of all illness.

Then come back and become "you" again. Say:

The end of illness
The promise of healing
I find solace
In the jewel of Tara
In the center of the lotus
Here I am I
The healing is mine
I give compassion and healing
I receive compassion and healing
From my heart
To my heart
We are one heart!
Om mani padme hum!

Stamp your feet. Clap your hands loudly like the sound of thunder at each direction and the center, each time saying:

Illness begone!
The healing now begins
Within and without
Phadt! Soha!

Ring the bell three times again, saying:

Tara Tara Tara!
Healing, balance, and freedom to all living beings!

Now put out the incense and pour the water into a potted plant or into the ground.

Go forth ever in the footsteps of Tara. You now have healing powers to heal yourself and others.

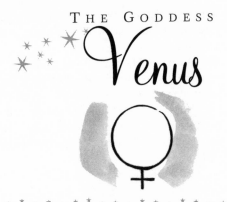

ORIGIN: Roman
ATTRIBUTES: beauty, love, and sexuality
COLOR: green or red/pink
SYMBOL: Venus symbol
ELEMENT: water
STONE/METAL: emerald or turquoise, copper, and gold coins
SCENT: Rose

INTRODUCTION

Venus is the great goddess to invoke if you want to bring real love into your life. No love spell is complete without her, and she is known to grant love to those who feel they have missed out before.

Venus is the famous Roman goddess of love, passion, and beauty. Her beauty is from within as well as outside. Generosity, kindness, and a loving nature are what she is all about. Centuries ago she began as an ocean goddess who "rose in beauty on a shell" to delight all the gods with love. Venus oozes seduction and passionate lust, and all of her images show a voluptuous, naked goddess glowing with love. It is no wonder that her priestesses were sacred prostitutes! Yet her true self is romantic or true love, that which unites spirit and body. Sometimes shown as a virginal goddess or Venus Pandemic (love for all) she renews herself after making love by bathing in the sea, and becoming a virgin again. True love, you see, is always new!

It is said that due to a break between the sky god and the earth mother, Venus was born from the foam of the sea, rising in beauty. Venus was blond-haired, blue-eyed, and voluptuous, and the winds carried her to the island of Cythera. Venus is also said to have been the wife of Hephaestus, the lover of Adonis, and the consort of Mars. Venus is known as queen of the sea and is also known by the name Mari or Marianna. The Greeks called her Aphrodite.

Venus was the mother of the Romans and mother of the city of Venice. The goddess Venus favors any type of sweet fruit, especially golden apples and strawberries. Venus is a water goddess and so the animals and birds sacred to her are the dolphin, swan, and heron. Her perfume is myrrh, which was burned at her temples by her priestesses. Roses are said to have sprung from her feet when she walked the earth. The goddess Juno borrowed her enchanted girdle in order to persuade her husband to pay attention to her. Her favored metal is copper, and one of her main temples was Paphos on Cyprus, the island named for its copper mine. Gold is also sacred to her, since her worshippers left gold coins after visiting her priestesses. The stones that she favors are turquoise and emeralds. Seashells of any kind are sacred to her, but scallop shells in particular are treasured. Venus's color is green, which is the same color as the heart chakra. And the Romans made Friday her special day.

Venus is love and the art of loving yourself as well as others. Call on her for love, or to find true love, or to love yourself more. Ah, Venus! Love, love, love!

* * * * *

GODDESS VENUS INVOCATION

O Venus !
Dea amare
Salve Venus!
O beautiful one with flowing hair and crimson lips
Curvy hips a lovely voluptuous body

Goddess of passionate lust for life
Insatiable desires and sensuous beauty
Radiance from within
Like the horses from the sea
You shine and sparkle
A billion emeralds.
Aphrodite, you glitter
Wondrous beauty for all eyes to behold
Graceful and loving
Gracious to all
Bestower of beauty
Emerge from the turbulent sea with
Waves crashing around you
Confident in your ability to love all
And to love yourself
Salve dea amare!
Venus, you are desirable!
The calm in the center of emotional storms,
Playful as the dolphin, graceful as a swan
A nature spirit and goddess of the ocean.
Seduction and passion are your guides
Your love has no boundaries
Beauty to all that you encounter
Lovely lady of the sea
I invoke thee!
I love you!
Fill me with *love*!
Mea voluptas
Deliciae meae
Venus celebrare!

★ ★ ★ ★ ★

Goddess Venus Visualization Exercise

You are standing on a white beach,
Blue sky above you.

Seagulls fly,
Cedar trees grip the rocks,
Beautiful shells around you,
All is beautiful and sunny!
Suddenly there is a great churning of the sea.
Suddenly
Beautiful Venus, naked and perfect
Rises from the foam of the sea.
You see her rise from the ocean, nude on a large scallop seashell
You are amazed at seeing beauty beyond compare.
Her long fair hair surrounds her
Covering her modestly.
She smiles at you,
And you and the world
Are filled with love.
She gestures and suddenly
You are surrounded by gently falling
Rose petals
And gold coins.
She bestows the gift
Of love for those who ask.
Your love shines like gold
And your aura radiates sunny rays,
Dolphins jump by your side;
Her playful nature entices them
When you gesture.
They swim near the shore
You ask her for
The forbidden fruit of love.
She hands you love with a smile,
A golden apple that you eat,
Filling your heart with love.

The water fowl come out to meet you.
Swans and herons,
They crane their necks to listen to your
Lovely voice, and to catch a glimpse of your smile.

Everyone is in the mood for mating.
With the goddess of love and delight before you,
You smell roses,
The scent of love!
No one is lovelier than she,
More beautiful or charming.
You whisper to her:
"Venus, O goddess of love
You have inspired artists by the score.
Inspire me now!
I worship your evening star,
O planet Venus,
Sparkling endlessly.
Into the twilight you shine
Like an eternal fountain.
You pour love over me!
Salve Venus!
Bonum dea!
Come now!
Surround me with love!
Bring true love to me!
Fiat Venus!"
And now the winds take you like a leaf.
You rise away from the beautiful goddess
Into the blue sky
Like a bird
And back to your world,
Filled with love!

★ ★ ★ ★ ★

$\mathcal{G}$ODDESS VENUS EMPOWERMENT RITUAL:
BECOMING LOVE, LOVE, LOVE
(ALL YOU NEED IS . . .)

The Goddess Venus will not only help you love yourself; she can guide you to find lasting love. Becoming Venus will give you the feeling that you are loved and cherished by others, even if life brings you down. Venus will help you reach the lasting love that you have desired your entire life, or, if you are in a long-term relationship, she will help you to renew it. Venus teaches that you too can rise from the ocean of life as a vision of beauty who attracts love. In ancient Rome, Venus priestesses became her by making love to the patrons of her temple. Dedicate every loving experience you have to bringing *more* love into your life in the name of Venus. You can never have too much love!

You Will Need
◉ a green cloth
◉ an image of Venus
◉ a little sea salt
◉ matches
◉ rose incense
◉ a red candle
◉ rose oil, as pure as possible
◉ a seashell (like the one you found on the beach
on your last vacation)
◉ a dozen red roses
◉ a turquoise ring or necklace
◉ sweet wine or apple juice
◉ some strawberries or red apples

The Ritual
Do this ritual at a seashore amidst pine trees if possible, or in a room filled with green pine or cedar branches and sunlight. It should be done on a Friday if possible. Lay everything nicely on the green cloth facing north. Meditate on love.

Toss a pinch of the sea salt around you counterclockwise to purify the space, saying:

Begone all that is not light and love!
Lux et amore!
Lux et amore!
Lux et amore!

Now say:

> *Bonum dea!*
> *Goddess of love*
> *Salve Venus*
> *Come to me now!*
> *You are the great goddess of love*
> *In Greece you were called Aphrodite*
> *In every language you are love*
> *The bringer of love*
> *The form of love*
> *Be here now!*
> *Venus fiat!*

Light the incense, face the North, and say:

> *You are a lovely goddess of love and beauty*
> *Shower me with a sea mist of purity*
> *Deep within me resides a wonderful*
> *Creature powerful intense of heart*
> *Seduction is my secret weapon*
> *Love of self is my jewel*
> *My eternal beauty lies within*
> *Salve Venus!*

Offer the incense to the East and say:

> *You are a lovely goddess of love and beauty*
> *Shower me with a sea mist of purity*
> *Deep within me resides a wonderful*
> *Creature powerful intense of heart*
> *Seduction is my secret weapon*
> *Love of self is my jewel*
> *My eternal beauty lies within*
> *Salve Venus!*

Offer the incense to the South and say:

> *You are a lovely goddess of love and beauty*
> *Shower me with a sea mist of purity*
> *Deep within me resides a wonderful*

> *Creature powerful intense of heart*
> *Seduction is my secret weapon*
> *Love of self is my jewel*
> *My eternal beauty lies within*
> *Salve Venus!*

Offer incense to the West, saying:

> *You are a lovely goddess of love and beauty*
> *Shower me with a sea mist of purity*
> *Deep within me resides a wonderful*
> *Creature powerful intense of heart*
> *Seduction is my secret weapon*
> *Love of self is my jewel*
> *My eternal beauty lies beneath*
> *Salve Venus!*

Now light the red candle and say:

> *Goddess of love and beauty!*
> *Bonum dea*
> *Dea amore!*
> *Bathe me with the light and water of love*
> *Deep within me you reside*
> *Goddess of powerful heart*
> *Seduction is your gift*
> *Love of self the jewel you give me*
> *You reveal my eternal beauty within*
> *Salve Venus!*

Disrobe. Anoint yourself with rose oil and beauty! Stand naked with a shell in one hand and a rose in the other. Feel the power of Venus filling you. Open your arms and see yourself rising from the ocean! Imagine standing upon a shell. You are like the sun, shining all around! *Be Venus!* Say:

> *I am the Goddess Venus!*
> *I accept myself for who I am*
> *I love my body the best that I can*
> *Others are drawn close to me,*
> *When I enter a room all is hushed.*

Who is this goddess of beauty and lust?
Deep within me I know that I project
An inner knowing that I am best.

I love myself and in turn love others
I envision beauty and light
All wondrous femininity and none of its plight
My secret is that I know that love is the beginning of understanding.

I see deep raising oceans
And all the bounties of the sea
I am a child of the foam when waves crash up
On the shore
Deep is my love of self and others,
Deeper than the ocean floor.

The tides rise and ebb
On the phase of the moon
Only I, Venus, never wane
Beauty, confidence, love
Is my forever domain.

I am so wonderful
That I can charm the
Birds out of the trees
The heron, the swan
That is as graceful as me
I am the Goddess Venus
Lovely as can be.

Roses spring from my feet
When I walk on Earth
Creatures fall in love
They cannot help it
I am so pretty and radiate love
And smile at all those that I meet.

I am the Goddess Venus
The Romans named their

Most beautiful city after me
Venice is the most romantic place.

I am the Goddess Venus
Known by my other name
The Romans honor me when
I walk along the shores of their
Islands.

Above me is the planet
Venus known for its
Beauty and its proximity
To the moon
It is here that I watch over the
Lovers and embrace
All that whisper my name
You may have heard my
Invocation perhaps when you
Were a child
It started out like this.

Star light star bright
First star that I see tonight.
I wish I may, I wish I might
Have the wish I wish tonight

I am not a star but a planet
And it is this planet Venus that
You call my name
I can give wishes to all
Especially the ones asking for love
I am Venus after all.

Now get ready to prepare the aphrodisiac. This will be useful for any time that you want to have love enter your life. Say:

I am Venus!
I am Dea Amare
And my love is strong

I am Love!
My potion is powerful and magickal
It can charm birds out of the sky
And fish out of the sea
One of my familiars is the dolphin
We are both playful
As is love.
My love is strong
My heat is complete
My desire goes beyond
All other gods!
I am the Goddess Venus
And all fall in love with me
When I rise from the sea
On the land or ocean
No one is lovelier then me!

Take up the ring or necklace, anoint it with oil, and put it on, saying:

Here I show the morningstar
I center my will
And project love as a jewel
May all see and know!
I am Venus!
The goddess of love
And my star shines within me
The water glows with phosphorus
Beneath me lies a heart of gold.
I give love freely and in turn
Love is given freely to me
I am the most enchanting goddess
I am Venus
I am Aphrodite
I am beautiful
I am in love
With myself
As well as others

All depend
On me for inspiration
I am the muse for many
Who are captivated
By my beauty and charm
Amore Fiat!

Now sit and meditate on being love. Feel all the kinds of love there are. Sink into an ocean of love and become the morningstar! When the power fades and you return to becoming "you," then slowly lay down the rose and shell. Dress again in green and drink some wine. Sprinkle a little out to Venus and say:

Honor to you, O Venus!
Goddess of beauty
Thank you, O goddess of love,
No man or woman can resist you!
Venus bless me
Now and forever
That I may give and get love
And manifest love
Across the earth
And over the ocean
Salve Venus!
Salve Bonum Dea!
Salve Amore!
Venus Fiat!

Now, blow out the candle and incense. Eat the strawberries and apples, or save them and offer them to your intended. Go and love and be loved in return!

THE GODDESS
Yakshi

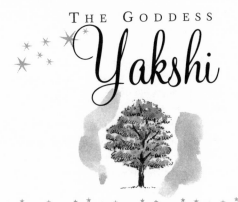

* * * * * * * * * * * * * * * * * * * *

ORIGIN: Hindu
ATTRIBUTE: protection and love of trees and wilderness
COLOR: brown and varied green
SYMBOL: tree
ELEMENT: earth
STONE/METAL: petrified wood or amber
SCENT: all tree resins or leaves

* * * * * * * * * * * * * * * * * *

INTRODUCTION

Are you a nature spirit or one who loves the great outdoors and whose heart beats faster when surrounded by trees, mountains, and wildlife? If you wish to get in touch with your wild spirit or simply want to become as wise and powerful as an ancient tree, Yakshi is the goddess who holds the green key for you!

Yakshi is an ancient Hindu goddess who personifies the spirit of the deep forest. Her origins reach far back to the beginnings of the Dravidian Indus River Valley culture many thousands of years ago. Some variants of her name are Yaksa, Yaksha, Yakkha, and Yakho. The root of *Yak* seems to be "nature," and the various endings mean divinity or spirit. Probably the most common name given to tree spirits is Yakshini (literally: "feminine nature spirit"). These tree spirits are much like the Greek dryads, and as such are accessible divinities for most humans. Their forms emerge from trees or are seen peering seductively from the underbrush with wild black eyes. Yakshi or Yakshini can be kind or mischievous, but are said to be intensely protective of trees and wildlife. They were said to sometimes lure unsuspecting travelers deep into the forest, but just as often they save or help those in need.

Yakshi is a full-bodied, sensuous goddess with a voluptuous figure, narrow waist, and large breasts. She is often depicted naked, surrounded by vegetation. She often stands bending as if in dance, one ankle crossing the other, with arms lost in tree limbs, facing the sky. The tree goddess may, in her most primal form, be an aspect of Durga, one of the great goddesses of nature. She is often shown with trees growing from her to feed the world. After saving all the gods by destroying demons, she vowed to reappear as Sakambari: the tree goddess. In her honor it is chanted "Plants O ye Mother, I hail you as goddess."

Ganesh, the elephant-headed god who became lord of the tree spirits, is the mate of Yakshini. Though the origins are ancient, even today some tales of the tree goddess survive. The archetypal hero Vijaya was wandering in the woods one night when Yakshi appeared as a beguiling and beautiful woman. She led him deep into the woods until he was lost, but she could not hurt him due to his magickal power. She then appeared in her true form as the tree goddess and he pursued her. Catching her, he seduced her and she fell deeply in love with him, and they married.

In temples Yakshi always appears on gates. Creeping branches, symbolic of the protective goddess, or sometimes the form of the Saptamatrika ("seven mothers") are found protecting and empowering portals to temples. Some believe the earth cycle is the gate, the tree of life that links us all together. As the most fundamental form of living "green energy" on the planet, the tree mother protects and fills all with the green life force. We call upon her unified force, the total life energy of all the forests of the Earth, to rise up and protect the tree devas so the Earth may survive, and we may become part of the lovely wilderness we hike, camp, and play in! May we understand the tree as universal gateway to understanding the great mother. Today she is used to enhance your wild nature and get the most out of outdoor recreation.

Invocation of the Goddess Yakshi

Here is rooted the tree of life
Enchanting maiden goddess of green
Stillness and birdsong
Graceful limbs and shadow smile
Lady of the forest
Primal mother of the deep-woods beginning
Sap-full breasts and shimmering leaves
You are the face of the earth.
I bring forth your green power
Rain forest dreamer grow
Within our sacred circle
Ya-kshi
Earth spirit
Ya-kshini
Tree spirit priestess
Ya-kho
Black-dwarf tree woman

Come through the trees
Wearing your many masks
Dancing the dance of the trees
Bending and swaying in the wind
Opening the way
Between twilight and sunrise
Between darkest night
And brightest day.

I call you by the ancient names
Vanadurga!
Vriddhamata!
Kuvanna!
Earliest of mothers loved by man
Bring us light and bring us joy,
Primal goddess unchanged from the beginning

Bring us power and bring us strength,
Sorceress mate of heroes
Bring us love and bring us will,
Om dum yakshi namah svaha!
Tree mother, make us one with wilderness!

There is nothing but the void
It is divided into light and darkness
Standing in the center is a tree.
It grows from the belly of the earth mother
She sleeps and smiles and gives birth
A snake of emerald climbs the tree
And the tree towers becoming large.
From the tree emerges a goddess
In her hands is the beating heart
Of the mother earth
About her neck is a living chain of emerald
Yakshi comes
Yakshi reveals
Yakshi abides
Om dum yakshi namah svaha!
Tree mother, make us one with wilderness!

Yakshi mata has seven faces
Her body is formed of seven stars
The tree has seven branches
The seven branches have seven fruit
Her soul is an emerald with seven facets.

Om dum yakshi namah svaha!
Crone of black soil and decomposition
Open the gate of awareness
Saptamatrika!
May I become the trees!

Om dum yakshi namah svaha!
Infant spark of seed and sowing
Open the gate of birth

Saptamatrika!
May I become the trees!

Om dum yakshi namah svaha!
Girl-goddess sprout of joy
Open the gate of dancing
Saptamatrika!
May I become the trees!

Om dum yakshi namah svaha!
Maiden of sapling weaver of dreams
Open the gate of vision
Saptamatrika!
May I become the trees!

Om dum yakshi namah svaha!
Great mother of the fruit of knowing
Open the gate of creation
Saptamatrika!
May I become the trees!

Om dum yakshi namah svaha!
Ancient elder of time and tide
Open the gate of evolution
Saptamatrika!
May I become the trees!

Seven stars become
One star with seven points
Shining here within the sacred grove
Yakshi goddess eternal
Cycle of birth and death embracing
Tree of wisdom and all life.
Increase our awareness of green birth
Unleash our joy at the green vision
Grant us the knowing of creation mystery
May I evolve as you have evolved
In peace and in beauty.

From the earth returning to the earth
Rooted in soil reaching to the sun
Eternal mystery
Ever-present companion
I rest under your branches
Open for understanding
Tree mother, make us one with wilderness!
Om dum yakshi namah svaha!

* * * * *

GODDESS YAKSHI VISUALIZATION EXERCISE

There is an island
And the flesh of Earth has formed upon it.
All is silence.
The sun begins to set on your left.
The full moon begins to rise on your left.
Grasses begin to grow on the island,
And stars begin to come out above you.
In the blue-green-turquoise twilight
A beam of light descends,
And it strikes the new land in front of you.
A seed drifts down in the light
And slides into the new soil.
Within seconds a new tree begins to sprout.
It grows into the sky.
The branches reach out
And wrap their twigs and buds
Around the planets in the sky.
The sun and moon
Are pulled glowing into the trunk,
And the roots reach into the ocean
And the deeper dark below the sea.

The tree forms the nexus between heaven and Earth.
The star and planet light

Rains down and is absorbed by the branches.
The thunder and rumbling energy
Of the deepest Earth rises up to nourish the roots,
And the light and the dark
Mingle, mix, meet, and merge
Between the sun and the moon,
Between the heavens and the Earth,
And suddenly all is glowing.
And the tree becomes a beautiful woman
With long dark green hair and black eyes,
A waiting smile and dark brown skin,
Beautiful and sensuous and commanding,
One ankle crossing the other,
Arms swept up and out into the branches.
She is the soul and being of the tree.
She is the primal tree goddess, the flesh of nature.
She smiles and the tree is filled with leaves.
She sighs and the tree is covered by flowers.
A perfume of sweetness and spice fills the air.
She shivers in ecstasy and the tree bears eleven fruits.
One at the top
Dries and falls at your feet.
It is a warm, brown, smooth divided nut.
You open it easily and eat the kernel.
It is sweet and fills you with pleasure.

Suddenly you feel your body changing.
Your arms grow into the sky.
They become branches and reach out,
And you wrap your twigs and buds
Around the planets in the sky.
The sun and moon
Are pulled glowing into your body,
Which has become a massive trunk,
And your feet become roots that reach into the ocean
And the deeper dark below the sea.

You have become the tree of life
 You form the nexus between heaven and Earth
The star and planet light
Rains down and is absorbed by your branches,
The thunder and rumbling energy
Of the deepest Earth rises up to nourish your roots,
And the light and the dark
Mingle, mix, meet, and merge
Between the sun and the moon,
Between the heavens and the Earth,
Within your heart—center—secret self—
And suddenly all is glowing.
And you become a beautiful goddess
With long dark green hair and black eyes,
A waiting smile and dark brown skin.
And you reach out with your mind.
You reach out with your roots.
You reach out with your branches.
And you touch and are filled by
The group mind of all trees.
You look around
And sense every tree in the world.
You hear the murmuring of every tree;
you smell the green life of every tree.
Suddenly you become one with the group-mind of all trees.
Your consciousness is filled with green.
You float in the tree-mind and feel peace.
Eventually you return to your body.
And you feel the branches fade away.
You feel the roots dissolve.
And you feel the mixture of light and dark within,
Absorbed into your body.
You are now seated in a familiar spot
Staring at a favorite tree.
You hug the tree,
Feel its bark and its life.

At your feet is a seed.
Put it in your pocket,
And say good-bye.
You and the tree are brothers,
And you will remember this
Every time you see a tree.

★ ★ ★ ★ ★

Empowerment Ritual of the Goddess Yakshi: Becoming the Seven Mother Forests — the Tree of Life

This ritual is for living as the green Earth and helping, healing, and enjoying the wildness of the forest, and wildlife and wilderness about you. Use this empowerment to connect with nature and the forests we love so much. Live like a tree walking!

You Will Need

◎ seven sticks from any local trees you feel are special

◎ a little fresh sap from any tree

◎ a glass of wine or water

◎ a small mirror

◎ some pine nuts

◎ a branch of any tree that is especially important for you

◎ a small spade or trowel

◎ a few flowers

The Ritual

Around a special tree in the forest gather all these items. Gather the seven sticks in a bundle and sweep the area counterclockwise, saying:

Out the damage
Out the pain
Out the evil and black rain
Out the poison
Out the ax
Out the fences

Out the tracks
Out the greed
Out the spite
Out the killing
In the light.

Cast a large circle in the opposite direction with the same branches bundled together, saying:

In the light
Of the trees
In the breath
Of the leaves
In the scent
Of the earth
In the green
Seeds give birth

Clap your hands three times, saying each time:

In the light of the trees
Yakshi, Yaksha, Yakshini!
Gam! Forest lord make it so!

Bless the altar area, the offerings, and yourself with a touch of sap and say:

Vanadurga! Kuvanna! Vriddhamata!
By the secret names
O mother of the forest I call you
You are the kind devas Punyajana
You are the consciousness of the tree mothers
Yakshi-Ma Yakshi-Ma Yakshi-Ma!
Bless, empower, and center this rite!
Dddddduuuuummmmmm!

Adya Yakshini Devata svaha!
Here is the blood of the mother Ya!
Here is the fire of Shakti life
Here is the glowing green tree nectar
The consciousness of the tree mothers

Yakshi-Ma! Yakshi-Ma! Yakshi-Ma !
Bless, empower, and center this rite!
Dddddduuuuummmmmm!

Drop some sap in the wine and swirl it. Drink it, then say:
Adya Yakshini Devata svaha!
Here is the milk of the mother Ya!
Here is the flowing rivers of Shakti life
Here is the dark water drawn up by roots
The consciousness of the tree mothers
Yakshi-Ma! Yakshi-Ma! Yakshi-Ma!
Bless, empower, and center this rite!
Dddddduuuuummmmmm!

Touch the sap to the mirror and breathe deeply, saying:
Adya Yakshini Devata svaha!
Here is the breath of the mother Ya!
Here is the wind of Shakti life
Here is the clear sparkling oxygen
The consciousness of the tree mothers
Yakshi-Ma! Yakshi-Ma! Yakshi-Ma!
Bless, empower, and center this rite!
Dddddduuuuummmmmm!

Smear some of the sap on the nuts and eat, saying:
Adya Yakshini Devata svaha!
Here is the flesh of the mother Ya!
Here is the physical body of Shakti life
Here is the seed-fruit nourishment
The consciousness of the tree mothers
Yakshi-Ma! Yakshi-Ma! Yakshi-Ma!
Bless, empower, and center this rite!
Dddddduuuuummmmmm!

Offer these things and your desire to become the tree spirit of the forest, saying these words:
Yaksha Yakkha Yakho Yakshini!
Mother of the forest salutations to thee!

Yaksh Mata
Great mother of trees
Flesh of beautiful wood
Hair of luxurious leaves
Legs and arms graceful as limbs
Bending down to whisper
Over a pond
As the wind flows through the forest
Black-eyed woman
Strong and joyful
Vibrant and mirthful
You are the one tree
The great tree at the beginning
The tree of life
The primal tree of first beginnings
Roots in the fiery center of magma
Branches enshrined about the galaxy
Daughter of stars
The sun and moon decorate your hair
And the serpent of the Earth
Is your girdle.

The tree is life
The tree is knowledge
The tree is growth
The tree is love
The tree is the center
Around which all turns
Tat Tvam Asi!
It is I.

Meditate and become the tree of life. Hold the special tree branch above you, and cross your ankles. Look up with pure joy, and become Yakshi, saying:

I am of the earth
Hum!
I am rooted in her heart

Hum!
I am weaving the sky
Hum!
I flow with the cycles of life
Hum!
I am born, I seed, I die
Hum!
I awake and reach out
Hum!
All become one
Hum!

As a tree, visualize all the trees in the world and reach out to them; become them. Lay out all of the seven branches you have been using before you. Take up each one of the seven branches, one at a time. As you read each verse below, pick up a branch and take upon yourself the green energy of each of the primal forests on Earth.

I am mother treespirit—I open the gate!
I am Yakshi Mata—I open the way!

The heart of forest—the soul of tree
Of North America—I am thee!
Ddduuummm!
The heart of forest—the soul of tree
Of Amazonia—I am thee!
Ddduuummm!
The heart of forest—the soul of tree
Of Central Africa—I am thee!
Ddduuummm!
The heart of forest—the soul of tree
Of Europa—I am thee!
Ddduuummm!
The heart of forest—the soul of tree
Of Siberia—I am thee!
Ddduuummm!
The heart of forest—the soul of tree
Of Sub-central Asia—let us be thee!

Ddduuummm!
The heart of forest—the soul of tree
Of Southeast Asia—let us be thee!
Ddduuummm!

You are Yakshi, the primal green goddess of wilderness! Become a tree, and say:

Trees are gathering
Trees are growing
Trees are whispering
Trees are showing
Joined together
Becoming as one
What long ago started
I again have begun!
Ya svaha!
Adya Yakshi Devata svaha!
I am the primal mother of trees
Adya Yakshi Devata svaha!
I am the primal mother of trees
Adya Yakshi Devata svaha!
I am the primal mother of trees

Maha Yakshina Devata svaha!

Meditate, eat the nuts, and drink the wine. Commune . . . let the forest teach and fill you as its purest power. When you are done and have returned to being "you," touch the tree before you, with both hands, saying:

The tree is life
The tree is knowledge
The tree is growth
The tree is love
The tree is the center
Around which all turns
Shanti Shanti Shanti
Om!

Toss each of the seven branches into the woods in a counterclockwise manner. Visualize each one as an arrow sending energy, love, and will to empower and heal each forested area. Say each time:

> *Heart of forest of North America—be well and be free!*
> *Heart of forest of Amazonia—be well and be free!*
> *Heart of forest of Central Africa—be well and be free!*
> *Heart of forest of Europa—be well and be free!*
> *Heart of forest of Siberia—be well and be free!*
> *Heart of forest of Sub-Central Asia—be well and be free!*
> *Heart of forest of Southeast Asia—be well and be free!*
> *Ddduuummm!*

Bury the rest of the nuts and sap at the base of the tree, leaving the flowers and your special tree branch on top. (Or keep that branch as a wand!) Then say:

> *Vanadurga! Kuvanna! Vriddhamata!*
> *By the secret names*
> *O mother of the forest I bid you good-bye*
> *May I always be*
> *The consciousness of the tree mothers*
> *Yakshi-Ma, bless, empower, and center us!*
> *That the power of the trees*
> *May always be with me*
> *Om dum Yakshi namah svaha!*
> *Heal the trees, heal the mother, heal the Earth!*
> *Svaha!*

Place the mirror in your pocket. This can be used on your next outdoor outing as a charm to reflect your wild spirit. Now leave, and realize that the great outdoors is to enjoy, not to endure.

About the Author

* ★ * ★ *

Sophia is a professional psychic, astrologer, and spiritual teacher with more than twenty-five years of experience, both in the United States and abroad. She was taught how to tap her psychic powers by her grandparents when she was a child. At the age of three she began her study of psychic reading, psychic healing, and spell casting. She has written a regular column called *Emerging Women* for the *New Times* and maintains a thriving practice as a professional reader and teacher. She currently carries on the family tradition in a yurt in a wooded corner of Seattle, Washington.